BUILDING
EFFECTIVE
LEARNING
COMMUNITIES

10302

BUILDING
EFFECTIVE
LEARNING
COMMUNITIES

Strategies for Leadership, Learning, & Collaboration

SUSAN SULLIVAN • JEFFREY GLANZ

CORWIN PRESS
A SAGE Publications Company
Thousand Oaks, California

This book includes material that is reprinted with the permission of AchieveGlobal, Inc.

For information:

Corwin Press
A Sage Publications Company
2455 Teller Road
Thousand Oaks, California 91320
www.corwinpress.com

Sage Publications Ltd.
1 Oliver's Yard
55 City Road
London EC1Y 1SP
United Kingdom

Sage Publications India Pvt. Ltd.
B-42, Panchsheel Enclave
Post Box 4109
New Delhi 110 017 India

Printed in the United States of America.

Library of Congress Cataloging-in-Publication Data

Sullivan, Susan.
Building effective learning communities: Strategies for leadership, learning, & collaboration / Susan Sullivan, Jeffrey Glanz.
    p. cm.
Includes bibliographical references and index.
ISBN 0-7619-3982-2 (cloth)—ISBN 0-7619-3983-0 (pbk.)
    1. School improvement programs—United States. 2. Educational leadership—United States. 3. Educational accountability—United States. I. Glanz, Jeffrey. II. Title.
LB2822.82.S844 2006
371.2—dc22   2005002540

This book is printed on acid-free paper.

05 06 07 08 09 10 9 8 7 6 5 4 3 2 1

Acquisitions Editor:	Robert D. Clouse
Managing Editor:	Elizabeth Brenkus
Editorial Assistant:	Candice L. Ling
Production Editor:	Laureen Shea
Copy Editor:	Carla Freeman
Typesetter:	C&M Digitals (P) Ltd.
Proofreader:	Christine Dahlin
Indexer:	Michael Ferreira
Cover Designer:	Rose Storey

Contents

Preface

It is time we had a new kind of accountability in education—one that gets back to the moral basics of caring, serving, empowering and learning.

—Hargreaves & Fullan (1998, p. 46)

Democratic schools in postmodern times require stronger leadership than traditional, top down, autocratic institutions. The nature of that leadership, however, is markedly different, replacing the need to control with the desire to support. Ironically, such leaders exercise much more influence where it counts, creating dynamic relationships between teachers and students in the classroom and resulting in high standards of academic achievement.

—Nadelstern, Price, & Listhaus (2000, p. 275)

The educational buzzwords since the 1990s have been "high academic standards" and "building collaborative learning communities." Most leaders and teachers have become all too aware that in reality, these concepts are very often oxymoronic. The press of national, state, and local accountability standards has placed enormous pressures on leaders, teachers, and students to provide measurable outcomes to meet everyone's standards. The hue and cry from administrators, teachers, parents, and students is increasing. The complaint is this: School is primarily focused on test preparation. Only reading and math count. Other subjects have been relegated to the back burner. A Florida elementary principal recounts how she eliminated the third grade art, music, and physical education programs that she believes are so important for children. She gave her third graders an extra 50 minutes of reading daily to make sure they wouldn't be retained, despite her disapproval of the state's mandatory retention policy. Scores rose but didn't meet the national standards because of a subgroup of special education students. So the school "failed" (Winerip, 2004a).

How can a collaborative learning community be built in this context? School has often become a race with the clock to become prepared for the next test. Where is the time that is so vital for building collaborative learning communities? Collaboration takes time, and time is a scarce commodity.

The goal of this book is to enable prospective and practicing school and district leaders, teacher and parent leaders, and other educational leaders to learn the skills and dispositions needed to create collaborative learning communities in which high academic standards are achieved for all members of the school community.

We propose a conceptual framework built on a series of assumptions emanating from two major premises. This framework will permit schools to join "high academic standards" with a "collaborative learning community." The centerpiece of this framework is *modeling reflective practice*. What, you might ask, has "modeling reflective practice" to do with "collaborative learning communities" and "high academic standards?" "Everything" is the response.

In this text, we will demonstrate how reflective practice underlies all the strategies and techniques for building learning communities and how the modeling of these practices by the leader(s), the teachers, and the children provides an enduring method for achieving strong academic and moral standards.

This volume offers the two parts of the equation that leaders and aspiring leaders need to build a high-achieving collaborative learning community:

- The tools for adults to understand and reflect on their learning and leading patterns
- The strategies and techniques to model and implement them with their staff and the other members of the learning community

What is unique and important about this text? The first section provides all the materials for leaders and aspiring leaders to learn first about themselves. The reader can choose which materials he or she thinks are suitable for the particular context and culture in which they will be used. These materials are appropriate to share with all adults in a school learning community. Many of these tools have adaptations for the K–12 classroom, and others can be adapted for classroom use. We believe that this personal knowledge is a prerequisite for acquiring the tools to build a learning community.

The second section presents a multitude of strategies and techniques to build a reflective learning community. Again, the reader can choose those he or she deems appropriate for the particular context. Most of them are adaptable for the K–12 classroom. This user-friendly text includes blank tools and techniques that can be replicated for professional development or in the classroom.

What is also distinctive in this book is the combination of the initial focus on individual development followed by strategies and techniques for group development. Many texts offer an array of communication and group development techniques, and others focus on a specific adult development orientation. None see the integration of personal development as the necessary step before attempting group development. The immersion of both facets in reflective practice seals in the effectiveness of this combination.

We would be remiss if we did not recommend some of the texts that focus entirely on adult and group development and on which we have drawn: *Reflective Practice for Educators* (Osterman & Kottkamp, 2004); *The Constructivist Leader* (Lambert, Walker, Zimmerman, Cooper, Lambert, Gardner, & Szabo, 2003); *Communicating in Small Groups* (Beebe & Masterson, 2000); *The Power of Protocols* (McDonald, Mohr, Dichter, & McDonald, 2003); *Schools That Learn: The Fifth Discipline Fieldbook for Educators, Parents, and Everyone Who Cares About Education* (Senge, Cambron-McCabe, Lucas, Smith, Dutton, & Kleiner, 2000); *Schools as Professional Learning Communities* (Roberts & Pruitt, 2003); *Finding Your Leadership Style* (Glanz, 2002); and *Let Me Learn* (Johnston & Dainton, 1997).

To lay the foundation for the two major sections of this book, an introductory chapter provides an overview of our perspective on constructivism and reflective practice. The first section on leadership and learning styles comprises Chapters 2 and 3. Each chapter begins with a set of reflective questions to begin your thinking about the content (about what you know about yourself and those around you). Reflective questions also follow chapter sections. They can be used as individual prompts, as share pairs, for online or group discussions, or for microlabs (see Chapter 7 for model). These chapters include mini–case studies also followed by reflective questions that draw on what you have learned in each chapter. Suggestions for practice and use in the university classroom and for professional development of the adult and student members of the school community conclude the two chapters. Every chapter closes with suggested readings to further and deepen knowledge.

Chapter 2, "Leadership and Self-Knowledge," focuses on the importance of self-knowledge for those engaged in leadership activities. Awareness of our identities helps determine how we understand and practice leadership and engage in relationships that are integral to it. Knowledge of our strengths and weaknesses, our personality preferences, what drives and motivates us, and the impact we have on others can influence our actions. Thus this chapter guides you in finding your personal leadership style. An emphasis on ethical and moral leadership distinguishes it from most leadership surveys. The chapter includes reflective activities that will assist you in sharing this guide to leadership and self-knowledge with your colleagues and even your students.

Chapter 3, "Let Us Learn," addresses the need for *all* learners to understand their internalized learning behaviors, the learner's actions, and the necessity of building a common vocabulary to communicate these learning processes. The author presents the *Let Me Learn* process that Christine Johnston developed from the interactive learning model. Johnston derived four patterned operations from Philip's (1936) work: Sequence, Precision, Technical Reasoning, and Confluence. Samples from the Learning Connections Inventory reveal how this inventory provides a framework for understanding one's learning behavior and responses in learning situations. Suggestions follow for use in the university classroom, with school leaders and teachers, parents, and children. The author recounts one of her personal experiences introducing the inventory and concludes with reflective questions about the use and value of the inventory in the readers' schools.

Based on the knowledge gained in the first chapters, Chapter 4 facilitates the development of the first draft of your leadership vision statement. The authors provide guidelines to start your thinking and provide a reflective format to develop your ideas with university colleagues or other school leaders. Sample statements are included to start the reflection process. Equipped with personal understanding of who you are as a leader and learner and how that knowledge is reflected in your leadership vision, you are prepared to tackle the skills needed to lead and participate in groups and teams. The second section of the book is divided according to the skills and strategies essential for effective meetings. Chapter 5 begins with an overview of communication skills and techniques that are prerequisites for effective meetings: Listening skills, barriers to communication, and sending assertion messages form the baseline of effective communication.

The next steps, "breaking the ice" and "getting started," form the basis of Chapter 6. Included in this chapter are suggested "icebreakers," which set the personal tone for meeting communication. The second section of this chapter offers a panoply of techniques to foster the building of a collaborative, productive environment. All of the suggestions in this chapter include adaptations to different environments and recommendations for classroom and/or site practice.

In Chapter 7, the authors cull together from their extensive combined experience fostering and teaching collaborative decision making a panoply of effective strategies, techniques, and exercises for making meetings work. The range is from corporate techniques such as force field analysis, rating scales, and systems thinking exercises to tuning protocols such as descriptive review and small-group consultancies. As a guarantee of their effectiveness, the authors have included only approaches that have personally worked for them. Guidelines for using these skills, reflective questions, vignettes to contextualize their appropriateness, and scenarios to practice them in the university classroom and on-site are provided.

Chapter 8, "Pulling It Together," tells the story of a district and school that created a learning community through the use of many of the processes described in the book. It concludes with reflective questions to facilitate the readers' reflections about their personal contexts.

CORWIN PRESS

The Corwin Press logo—a raven striding across an open book—represents the union of courage and learning. Corwin Press is committed to improving education for all learners by publishing books and other professional development resources for those serving the field of K–12 education. By providing practical, hands-on materials, Corwin Press continues to carry out the promise of its motto: **"Helping Educators Do Their Work Better."**

Acknowledgments

We would like to thank the graduate students at the College of Staten Island, Wagner College, and the many school leaders, leadership teams, and teams of teachers in the New York area with whom we have developed and used these ideas and strategies.

Susan Sullivan would also like to thank Karen Osterman, Bob Kottkamp, and Ruth Silverberg for their ongoing shared reflections on reflective practice and learning that have enriched her thinking. She would also like to thank her colleague and friend Vivian Shulman, who has served as a sounding board, reader, and reflector on all of her recent work.

Jeffrey Glanz would also like to thank Steve Kuntz and Grace Ibanez-Friedman of St. John's University for their partnership and collaboration on the Annual Reflective Practices conferences cosponsored by St. John's and Wagner College. He would also like to acknowledge and thank Scott Miller, Joe Martucci, Karina Constantino, and Vincinza Gallassio, whose insights helped the author bridge theory to practice.

Corwin Press would like to thank the following peer reviewers for their contributions:

Kermit Buckner, Professor and Chair
Department of Educational Leadership
College of Education
East Carolina University
Greenville, North Carolina

Christi Buell, Principal
Poplar Grove School
Franklin, Tennessee

Robert Calfee, Distinguished Professor
Graduate School of Education
University of California
Riverside, California

Kay Harmless, Executive Director
Indiana Principal Leadership Academy
Indiana Department of Education
Indianapolis, Indiana

Thom Loomis, Principal
Arcadia High School
Arcadia, Ohio

Gary McCartney, Superintendent of Schools
South Brunswick Township Public Schools
Monmouth Junction, New Jersey

About the Authors

 **Susan Sullivan** received her BA from Elmira College, her MAT from The Johns Hopkins University, and her MEd and EdD from Teachers College, Columbia University. She served as an instructor in the Department of Romance Languages of The Johns Hopkins University for 10 years and as a teacher and administrator in Baltimore, Maryland; Rome, Italy; and the New York City area. She is currently Chair of the Department of Education of the College of Staten Island, The City University of New York. She was Coordinator of the Program in Educational Administration and continues to teach graduate courses in supervision of instruction and educational leadership. Her current research interests center on reflective practice, the role of the school district in systemic change, and supervision of instruction and its alternatives. She and Jeffrey Glanz have just completed the second edition of their book *Supervision That Improves Teaching: Strategies and Techniques.* They also have a staff development book, *Supervision in Practice,* and an accompanying video. Susan Sullivan has also published in journals such as *The Journal of School Leadership, The Journal of Supervision and Curriculum Development, Education and Urban Society, The International Journal of Leadership in Education,* and *Educational Leadership and Administration: Teaching and Program Development Journal.*

Jeffrey Glanz, EdD, currently serves as Dean of Graduate Programs and Chair of the Department of Education at Wagner College in Staten Island, New York. He also coordinates the educational leadership program that leads to New York State certification as a principal and assistant principal. Prior to arriving at Wagner, he served as executive assistant to the president of Kean University in Union, New Jersey. Dr. Glanz held faculty status as a tenured professor in the Department of Instruction and Educational Leadership at Kean University's College of Education. He was named Graduate Teacher of the Year in 1999 by the Student Graduate Association and was also that year's recipient of the Presidential Award for Outstanding Scholarship. He served as an administrator and teacher in the New York City public schools for 20 years. Dr. Glanz has authored, coauthored, and coedited 13 books and has more than 35 peer-reviewed article publications. With Corwin Press, he coauthored the best-selling *Supervision That Improves Teaching* (2nd ed.) and *Supervision in Practice: Three Steps to Improve Teaching and Learning;* and he authored *The Assistant Principal's Handbook* and *Teaching 101: Strategies for the Beginning Teacher.* Most recently, Dr. Glanz has authored the *What Every Principal Should Know About Leadership: The 7 Book Collection*, which includes the following titles: *What Every Principal Should Know About Instructional Leadership, What Every Principal Should Know About Cultural Leadership, What Every Principal Should Know About Ethical and Spiritual Leadership, What Every Principal Should Know About School-Community Leadership, What Every Principal Should Know About Collaborative Leadership, What Every Principal Should Know About Operational Leadership,* and *What Every Principal Should Know About Strategic Leadership.* Consult his Web site for additional information: http://www.wagner.edu/faculty/users/jglanz/web/.

About the Contributor

Ruth Powers Silverberg has served schools and programs as a teacher and leader for more than 25 years and is currently the coordinator of the Post Master's Certificate Program for Leadership in Education at the College of Staten Island, CUNY. Dr. Silverberg earned her doctorate in educational administration from Hofstra University after teaching music in public and private schools in upstate New York, Long Island, and New York City. She continues to conduct research in her primary area of interest: relationships in schools and their influence on children's and adults' learning.

*Susan Sullivan would like to dedicate this book to her
mother and to the memory of her father. Their unfaltering love
for learning, their positive spirits, and steadfastness in all
their pursuits combined with their love paved the way for their children.*

*Jeffrey Glanz would like to dedicate this book to all educators who are
committed to the hard but rewarding work of building collaborative learning
communities. He reminds them all that "failure is the first step toward success."*

PART I

Preparing for Leadership: Focusing on the Personal

1

Reaching Our Common Goal

High Achievement for All Children

In a high-stakes context, school leaders must search for ways to create a culture of high expectations and support for all students and a set of norms around teacher growth that enables teachers to teach all students well.

—Linda Lambert (Lambert et al., 2003, p. 2)

Reflective Questions*

1. What are some of the values, beliefs, and dispositions that you think are needed in a learning community?

2. How do you feel the standards movement has affected your school's climate or school climate in general?

(Continued)

AUTHOR'S NOTE: Throughout the book, reflective questions or reflective practice suggestions will be interspersed. These questions can be addressed in several ways. The students can write their reflections individually or discuss them with their neighbors (pair-share). The instructor can create a synchronous or asynchronous online discussion, divide the class into groups and discuss, and/or set up microlabs (see Chapter 7 for directions in class or online).

(Continued)

3. Where do you think high-stakes testing has the greatest
   impact? Why? And how?

4. What do you think is the relationship between high-stakes
   testing and reflective practice?

Despite different philosophical and political orientations, we can
say that all educators and politicians presently voice agreement
on one principle: the primacy of high expectations and achievement for all of our children. And most agree that performance-
based accountability is necessary for large-scale improvement in
achievement and improvement in school quality across the board
(Elmore, 2003). The differences begin to surface when the discussion turns to how to reach this goal. On the government side, almost
all states established standards for student learning and testing
systems to assess achievement in the 1990s. Many urban districts,
for example, Chicago and New York City (Herszenhorn, 2004;
Steinhauer, 2004), recently chimed in, advocating for an end to
social promotion and the use of standardized tests to retain
students. In 2001, the federal government arrived on the scene at
full throttle with the No Child Left Behind Act (NCLB), placing the
single measure of standardized testing at the center of student
improvement and achievement.

The hue and cry that we discuss in this chapter derives from three
sources:

- Schools that are buckling under the pressures for accountability
- Parents who observe their stressed-out children
- Scholars who struggle to defend their beliefs in reflective prac-
  tice and constructivist teaching methods

We will begin with a few reports of the dilemmas created by the
"one-test accountability" movement. We will then present background
on reflective practice and constructivism. These two concepts underlie the practices that we believe can enable schools to meet the common goal of achievement for all children without sacrificing a quality
pedagogical environment for adults and children.

Children, Parents, and Their Schools in the Era of Accountability

The media are replete with stories of the sleepless nights of young children the days before the "big test," and the declaration of the "failure" of schools based on one measure: standardized tests. Our goal is to share some of the tensions that result from a high-stakes standardized testing environment and then focus on the ideas and means to build a different leadership climate. The deep and shared learning we propose ensures long-term achievement for adults and children. We believe that this timeless approach to leading and learning can succeed in whichever shifting sands you may be forced to navigate.

Making Leaps But Still Labeled as Failing

This title of a recent newspaper article is about a veteran principal's struggle to help the children in her school meet state and federal standards. The principal has compromised her educational principles to avoid holding third graders back. Despite her belief that "children need to play and sing and draw," she eliminated the third-grade music, art, and physical education programs to provide an extra 50 minutes of reading every day. The school went from a C to a B on the state report card system. The schoolwide reading and math scores also met federal standards, but the school was labeled "failing" under the NCLB system. The special education subgroup scores were too low despite the school's Herculean efforts. The principal concluded, "The teachers work so hard; the kids work so hard. It's discouraging to be told you're failing" (Winerip, 2004a, p. B9).

City Tests Loom and Third Graders Feel the Heat

In 2004, the New York City mayor introduced a new promotion policy. Third graders who scored at the lowest of four rankings in reading or math would not be promoted. As the tests drew near, it was reported that "teachers, parents and third graders across the city spoke of sleepless nights, butterflies in their stomachs and not a few tears" (Herszenhorn & Gootman, 2004, p. B2). One parent commented, "She's crying at night. . . . The poor kid's like a frazzle. She dropped off the softball team. Something had to give" (p. B2). Another parent commented, "Not only are the teachers feeling the pressure, but the children are feeling the pressure and the parents are becoming lunatics because all they are thinking about is this test" (p. B2). The extra preparation outside of class recalls SAT preparation: private costly classes on Saturdays, extra test preparation before and after school, private tutors, and 15,000 children attending spring vacation classes in the public schools. Parents and teachers reported that in many cases, drilling for the exams preempted regular school-work. Need we say more?

Principal Sees Mistake in Plan to Hold Back Third Graders

A 26-year-veteran New York City principal explained why he felt the 2004 third-grade retention policy was a "big mistake" (Winerip, 2004b, p. B9). In one of the city's poorest schools, he has third graders whose scores on the citywide reading test are the lowest: "1." And every year, thanks to all kinds of extra programs the school provides, most of the third graders who scored "1" are transformed into fourth-grade "3s" and "4s." Retention in his school does not make sense, because his students are divided into reading groups according to their abilities; there are fourth graders reading seventh-grade books and some reading second-grade books. Outside funding and grants support computer hardware and software programs that permit children to move at their own pace, no retention necessary. What the principal has found is that "you have to make the decision based on best interest of the child, not best interest of the bureaucracy" (Winerip, 2004b, p. B9).

Reflective Practice

Discuss with your neighbor two examples of the effects of standardized testing on your professional life or in your school.

Try to provide one positive example and one negative. Explain and support your choices.

The most important observation we can make from these examples, from those a host of others practitioners recount, and from federal, state, and district mandates is that high-stakes testing as an assessment measure is here to stay, at least for a while. These vignettes also reveal one of the greatest dangers in the focus on standardized tests: the reduction or elimination of individual- or school-based instructional choices. What we offer is not an alternative; it is a foundation upon which meaningful (effective), child-oriented school decision making can be based, no matter what the "forces from above" impose. This foundation is built from reflective practice and constructivist learning practices.

Reflective Practice

Reflective Questions*

1. How would you define reflection?

2. What opportunities do you give your students to reflect?

   How do they respond?

3. When does your faculty have the opportunity to reflect?

   What happens?

4. What impedes reflection in your life?

   What promotes it?

5. Do you think reflection is important?

   If so, why? If not, why not?

---

*NOTE: A class or online microlab would be a particularly appropriate forum for these questions.

The first level of this foundation is *reflective practice*. We believe that leaders who personally apply and model reflective practice, cultivate it among their staffs, and then develop these thought processes in their students build the first level of a sound decision-making model for their learning communities.

We also maintain that reflective practice underlies effective leading, teaching, and learning at all levels. All of the approaches, strategies, and techniques in this book begin with reflective practice as the underlying framework. We agree with Osterman and Kottkamp, who "believe firmly that reflective practice is an important and effective change process that is integral to the learning organization" (2004, p. x).

What are the assumptions of reflective practice that form the core of this book and that will assist in building a learning organization?

- It is a professional development and a problem-solving strategy.
- It is based on a belief that organizational change begins with individuals.
- It proposes that our actions and behavior depend much less on our "espoused" or conscious theories than on our "theories-in-use" or our deep tacit beliefs and assumptions.
- It is ultimately a way for educators to search for ever-improved ways to facilitate student learning. (Osterman & Kottkamp, 2004)

Although reflective practice contains other assumptions, we feel that those that we have highlighted are the most important for deep, long-lasting individual and schoolwide growth.

Reflective Questions

1. When do you think people feel a need to learn?

2. What makes you resist change?

3. What encourages you to embrace an innovation?

4. What does "walking one's talk" mean?

5. What do the above questions have to do with children's learning?

Espoused Theories and Theories-in-Use

To appreciate how an understanding and use of the concepts of espoused theories and theories-in-use in the school building can impact teaching and learning, we continue with what has often become the primary school focus: improving test scores.

One way to "prove" that all children can learn and improve is through standardized test scores. Many schools are focusing their efforts to improve achievement on (a) drilling students on the information needed for local and state tests and (b) teaching test-taking skills. The teachers give practice tests regularly, creating homework assignments and tests in the same format as the "real" tests, basically using the tests as the goal of teaching. In high-achieving schools, less time needs to be spent preparing for the tests. In struggling schools, little time is left after drilling.

We concur that raising test scores does indicate enhanced skills in the area being assessed and improves test-taking knowledge. What standardized tests do not address is instilling a love for learning. We believe that understanding the concepts of "espoused theories" and "theories-in-use" can influence how teachers work with each other and with children.

Osterman and Kottkamp (2004) have created an exercise that they call "The Problematic Student," which allows teachers to learn how they actually deal with a "problematic" person, as opposed to how they say or think they do. Our ability to understand and work with all of our students may be the best predictor of their success. Rather than improving achievement scores for the year, we can create "lifelong learners" who can improve every year, with or without our support. The exercise, which is described in more detail in the Resource section, is deceptively simple:

1. Identify a problematic student or person in your life. Note the problematic behavior, and indicate how you would prefer the person to be.

2. Observe the person in as many different settings as you can.

3. Describe what you learned about the person, yourself, and your attitudes (or mental models) toward this person. (Osterman & Kottkamp, 2004)

When one of the authors first assigned this exercise to her leadership students, she chose to observe her own interactions with one of her leadership candidates whom she found "problematic." The student was highly participative—so participative that she dominated discussions. Other students got bored and impatient, but it was difficult to intervene in a polite manner. The candidate's written work was also problematic, vague, and discursive. The author was frustrated and felt that she was more than patient. Much to her surprise, another candidate mentioned to the author that the student felt that the professor did not like her. So, the author decided to observe herself and the student as objectively as possible. She noticed a visible impatience on her own part and a tendency to avoid the student. The student, on the other hand, cheerfully participated, communicated with other students, and attempted to address her written work with the professor. The author consequently changed her overt attitude toward the student, whose behavior and responses immediately took on another tone. The candidate volunteered to help in a special project, explained the difficulties she had had with her written work, and made revisions.

This situation could have taken place with a teacher at any level and a colleague or student of any age. It reveals how student success often hinges on our deep understanding of our behavior and actions, rather than on our professed beliefs. It also can bring to light information about a student's needs and abilities that can result in longer-lasting outcomes than an improved standardized-test score.

Thus what we profess and say we believe, our "espoused theories," are often not congruent with what we do, our "theory-in-use."

Reflective Questions

1. Recount an experience where you were told that you acted in a manner that was inconsistent with your intentions.

   How did you respond to the observation?

   What were the consequences of this experience?

2. Have you ever suggested to someone that his or her behavior was inconsistent with his or her expressed beliefs?

   What was the reaction of the person?

   How did the interchange conclude?

3. What did you learn from these experiences?

Espoused theories are what we are able to say we think and believe. "They exist at a conscious level and they change with relative ease in response to new information" (Osterman & Kottkamp, 2004, p. 9). Since these theories are explicit, all we have to do is ask the person what he or she knows or believes. Our schoolhouses are filled with espoused theories: the mission statement on every classroom door, the classroom rules the students can recite, even the Pledge of Allegiance. How many of these espoused beliefs are enacted in the day-to-day activities of the school? Leaders surrounded by constant crises, emergencies, and problems that needed to be solved yesterday often feel obliged to rule by fiat or just do not have the time to delegate or think of a collaborative strategy. Teachers concerned about "covering" curriculum, preparing for tests, and dealing with challenging children are often hard-pressed to apply the strategies they embraced at the university or at the last professional development conference.

Why do the best of our intentions get sidelined? Why do we end up "teaching the way we were taught" and bringing up our own children the way we were raised? Our *theories-in-use* can clarify some reasons. Osterman and Kottkamp (2004) have summarized what these theories-in-use are and how we acquire them:

> Unlike espoused theories that develop through conscious and intentional thought, theories-in-use develop through acculturation. As we grow from infants to adults, society shapes our understanding of how the world works. Just as traditional societies pass on understandings about childbirth, family, natural forces, and the relationship of human beings to the cosmos, so too does our culture transmit, through the daily processes of living, interpretations of the world that shape our behavior. As adult members of that society, we no longer focus consciously on many aspects of our organizational behavior; we function by rote, doing what others have done before us. We may be unable to articulate the reasons for our actions; we may also lack full awareness of what we're doing and its effects. (p. 10)

Reflective Questions

1. Can you think of any of your teaching practices that may have roots in the way you were taught?

   Were you aware of their origins?

   Do you find them effective?

   Does this awareness raise any questions about their use?

2. What customs or behaviors do you see originating from your family?

   Which would you like to pass on to another generation?

   Which ones would you like to change?

3. What are some of the practices in your school that are consistent with the espoused theories?

   Which ones are inconsistent? Why?

   Have there been attempts to foster consistency between theory and practice? What happened?

Now that we are aware of the difficulties of practicing what we preach, what can we do? And why should we do it?

Change and learning occur when a problem or question exists for which one seeks a solution or answer. This simple sentence underlies our belief that reflective practice lies beneath meaningful learning in a school. Administrative, pedagogical, and learning questions and problems are effectively addressed through the reflective-practice process.

The process itself is based on experiential learning theory. Dewey (1938) explained that learning or inquiry begins with a problematic or indeterminate situation. The "KWL" (What I KNOW, What I WANT to Know, What I LEARNED) charts that so many teachers use provide a simple schema of how learning occurs: The student knows something, but the knowledge is incomplete or problematic. The teacher first explores with the students what they already *know*. The list allows them to see their present knowledge and to question information about which they are not sure. Then, the teacher asks the students to determine *what they want to learn*. How can we answer the questions, solve the problem, complete the knowledge? The third part pulls together what has been *learned*. The KWL cycle, however, is a linear process, whereas the reflective practice process is cyclical (see Table 1.1).

Table 1.1   KWL Chart

Social Studies: France		
What We Know	*What We Want to Find Out*	*What We Have Learned*
1. It is a country.	1. What's the climate like?	1. It varies from cool and rainy in the North to warm and sunny in the South.
2. It is located in Europe.	2. What kind of government do they have?	2. It is a parliamentary democracy with a prime minister and a president elected for six years.
3. Europe is a continent.	3. Where does "French toast" come from?	3. Since the French have always eaten a lot of bread and most used to live on farms, they dipped their stale bread in eggs and milk and fried it.
4. The people speak French.	4. What religion do the people practice?	4. It is a secular country. Most people are Catholic, but there are many Muslims, Jews, and Protestants.

NOTE: Just imagine all the fascinating conversations and a whole new set of questions that could ensue from four simple questions.

The reflective practice process begins as follows:

Stage 1: A *concrete experience* or *identification of the problem.* As Dewey described, it can be a problematic or indeterminate situation or an unsettling or troubling situation. What is essential is that inquiry leading to new information and knowledge is required.

Stage 2: *Observation and analysis.* Data collection takes place. Whether the "researcher" is looking at deepening knowledge or trying to resolve a personal or interpersonal situation, information is gathered from as many sources as possible. *Analysis* of the information or data leads to hypotheses or the third stage.

Stage 3: *Abstract reconceptualization* is a different or new perspective of the problem or enhanced knowledge.

Stage 4: *Active experimentation* completes this cycle. As differentiated from KWL, it assumes that the new theory, knowledge, or hypothesis has to be tested. Once new ideas or behaviors are enacted or tried out, adjustments or new questions emerge, thereby necessitating the beginning of a new cycle. (Osterman & Kottkamp, 2004)

At this juncture, we have provided a very general description of reflective practice that can apply to all learners. Osterman and Kottkamp (2004) have focused their framework on adults. We believe that reflective practice's positioning within experiential learning, situated cognition (Bridges, 1992), and, more recently, constructivism (Fosnot, 1993; Lambert et al., 2003) validates its use as a model for adults and children.

Reflective Questions

1. If you have used the KWL cycle, provide an example of an effective cycle and why it worked.

2. Discuss an ineffective cycle and why it didn't work.

   How could you have improved it?

3. What other problem-solving cycles are you familiar with?

   How are they set up?

   What has been effective or ineffective in their use? Provide examples.

Figure 1.1   Reflective Practice: An Experiential Learning Cycle

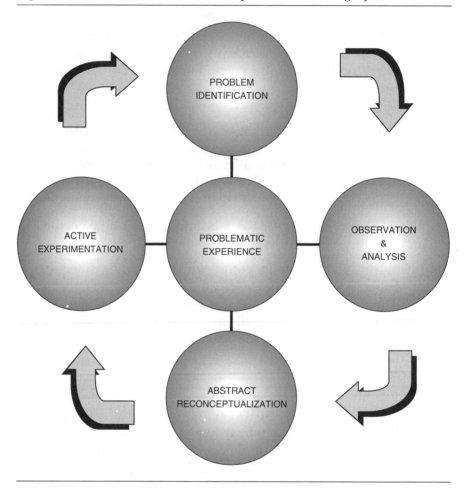

SOURCE: Osterman and Kottkamp, *Reflective Practice for Educators, Second Edition.*
Copyright © 2004 by Corwin Press. Reprinted with permission.

Constructivism and Reflective Practice

An empowered teacher is a reflective decision maker who
finds joy in learning and in investigating the teaching/learning
process—one who views learning as construction and teaching as a facilitating process to enhance and enrich development. (Fosnot, 1989, p. xi)

So many definitions of "constructivism" exist today that it is difficult to
figure out what it is, what it does, and how to view it. Von Glasersfeld
(1997) described it as a "vast and woolly area in contemporary
psychology, epistemology, and education" (p. 204). The origins of

constructivism stem from the theorists in 20th-century psychology whom we all studied in our psychology, educational psychology, and sometimes even philosophy classes: Piaget, Vygotsky, Kohler, Bruner, Dewey, and others.

Psychological or Individual Constructivism

Piaget is the best-known theorist of psychological or individual constructivism. He focused on meaning as the individual constructs it. He proposed that individuals pass through six cognitive stages. Thinking at each stage builds upon knowledge and thoughts acquired in the previous stage.

Social Constructivism

Vygotsky (1934/1986, 1978) is the best-known theoretician of social constructivism. He argued that since knowledge is constructed in a sociocultural context, social interaction, cultural tools, and activity shape individual development and learning. According to some scholars (Woolfolk & Hoy, 2003), Vygotsky bridges these two main branches: social and individual. "By participating in a broad range of activities with others, learners appropriate (take for themselves) outcomes produced by working together" (Woolfolk & Hoy, 2003, p. 91). Since Vygotsky was primarily interested in the development of the individual, some psychologists classify him as an individualist, while the sociocultural focus convinces others that he was a social constructivist. We agree with Woolfolk and Hoy's conclusion that Vygotsky bridged both camps.

Vygotsky's most well-known concept, the zone of proximal development (ZPD), is an example of the blending of the social and individual. On one hand, the ZPD development demonstrates how the learner mediates and negotiates knowing; the learner stretches just enough to construct new knowledge slightly above the current level of knowledge (Zepeda, 2000). On the other hand, it is with the support of another that the problem is solved.

Our favorite example of the ZPD is the ring toss game that the Efficacy Institute (Howard, 1987) uses in its seminars on development. Participants are given several rings and the stand on which to toss them. The goal is to figure out how to get the highest number of rings on the target. It is solving a problem, learning a new task. No other directions are given. Some choose to stand so far away that none of the rings land on the target. No learning occurs because the approach is unrealistic. Others choose to stand almost on top of the stand so that all the rings make it onto the stand. No learning occurs because no challenge exists. The facilitator then guides the group to stand just far enough away so that it becomes a challenge, but not an impossibility, for some of the rings to make it. The participants can actually feel the learning process as they refine their aim. Individual development takes place with the guidance of a more able peer or adult.

We can also distinguish the four stages of reflective practice in this example:

Stage 1: *Identification of the problem:* The participants must decide how to get the most rings onto the center of the stand.

Stage 2: *Observation and analysis:* The participants experiment with various strategies and analyze which work and which do not.

Stage 3: *Abstract reconceptualization:* The facilitator guides the participants toward a strategy that allows for success and also challenges (the ZPD).

Stage 4: *Active experimentation:* The participants try the new strategy, and the cycle can begin again.

The above exercise, a vivid example of the intersection of reflective practice and constructivism, is also very effective as a learning tool for children. What better way for children to learn about setting realistic but challenging goals?

The ring toss game also exemplifies social constructivism played out in a larger context, in which culture creates cognition or learning when the teacher uses tools and practices from the culture to steer the learner toward goals the culture values. In turn, the learning creates culture as the learners construct new practices and solutions that are incorporated into the culture (Serpell, 1993).

It is this dual concept of individual and situated or social learning that is so integral to our conception of constructivism. Reflective practice permits the leaders and the teachers to construct the self-knowledge that facilitates the creation of the school culture. If all the adults in the school community are involved in this individual and social learning, they can then proceed to incorporate the children in the reflective, constructivist learning process. Almost all of the processes presented in this book can be used or adapted for K–12 classroom use.

Osterman and Kottkamp (2004, p. 16) have summarized best how learning through reflective practice draws from constructivism, experiential learning, and situated cognition:

- Learning is an active process requiring involvement of the learner. Knowledge cannot simply be transmitted. For learning to take place, professionals must be motivated to learn and have an active role in determining the direction and progress of learning. Meaningful problems engage people in learning.
- Learning must acknowledge and build on prior experiences and knowledge. Accordingly, professionals need opportunities to explore, articulate, and represent their own ideas and knowledge.
- Learners construct knowledge through experience. Opportunities to observe and assess actions and to develop and test new ideas facilitate behavioral change.
- Learning is more effective when it takes place as a collaborative rather than an isolated activity and in a context relevant to the learner.

Reflective Questions

1. Can you think of a situation where you took an unrealistic risk?

   What happened?

2. Try to think of a time where you chose to stay in the very safe zone.

   What were the consequences?

3. Which of the three behaviors (very safe, moderate risk, extreme risk) best characterize(s) your approach to your work? Explain.

   Which characterize(s) your personal life? Explain.

4. Identify one area of your personal life and one from your professional life where you might use this type of analysis in your decision making.

The Outside Perspective

It is clear that we see reflective practice and constructivism across the entire school community as the basis of the learning community. The goal of this book is to provide school leaders—a role that can span the school community—with the knowledge and skills to create this reflective, collaborative environment. Some of you may be concerned that this type of individual and social reflecting and construction of knowledge may be a passing phenomenon limited to the world of education. Disciplines outside of education can give us insight into current organizational and business perspectives on organizational learning. These points of view can either support our ideas or bring them into question.

We have found that the extensive interest in the "information society" and in the "knowledge economy" has not lessened the importance that business and organizational scholars attribute to how learning occurs. We are including some quotations from business and organizational scholars that resonate with our ideas:

> Knowledge is always a process, and a relational one at that, which cannot therefore be located simply in an individual head, to be extracted and shared as an organizational asset. Knowledge is the act of conversing, and learning occurs when ways of talking, and therefore patterns of relationship change. . . . The knowledge assets of an organization lie in the pattern of relationships between its members. (Stacey, 2001, p. 98)

Some organizational researchers explicitly link what they call "communities of practice" to the knowledge economy. Whether implicit or explicit, reflective practice is an integral part of the community of practice:

> Companies at the forefront of the knowledge economy are succeeding on the basis of communities of practice, whatever they call them. . . . Communities of practice are groups of people who share a concern, a set of problems, or a passion about a topic, and who deepen their knowledge and expertise in this area by interacting on an ongoing basis. (Wenger, McDermott, & Snyder, 2002, p. 4)

Michael Fullan (2003) has culled Brown and Duguid's (2000) ideas about a knowledge community and created a list of their beliefs about the effective use of knowledge:

- Knowledge lies less in its databases than in its people. (p. 121)
- For all information's independence and extent, it is people, in their communities, organizations, and institutions, who ultimately decide what it all means and why it matters. (p. 18)

- A viable system must embrace not just the technical system but also the social system—the people, organizations, and institutions involved. (p. 60)
- Knowledge is something we digest rather than merely hold. It entails the knower's understanding and having some degree of commitment. (p. 120)

Learning communities are clearly not unique to the world of education. Gladwell's (2000) prescription for changing people's beliefs and behavior is completely consistent with the current educational thoughts about schools:

To bring about a fundamental change . . . that would persist and serve as an example to others, you need to create a community around them, where these new beliefs could be practiced, expressed, and nurtured. (p. 173)

Envisioned change will not happen or will not be fruitful until people look beyond the simplicities of information and individuals to the complexities of learning, knowledge, judgment, communities, organizations, and institutions. (p. 213)

The following vignette addresses Gladwell's idea about bringing about fundamental change in a community where teachers look at "the complexities of learning, knowledge, judgment, communities, and organizations" (p. 213). This case also exemplifies how reflective practice and constructivist learning can be practiced in an urban school where teachers are implementing mandated curricula.

Literacy and the Ring Toss Game

In the mid- and late 1990s, a number of school districts around the country, and in particular large urban ones, contracted with Jeffrey Howard's "Efficacy Seminar" to explore with teachers their beliefs about development of children and then to generate a plan to improve the academic performance of their students. As mentioned earlier in the chapter, Vygotsky's zone of proximal development (ZPD) played an important part in the Efficacy Seminar's ideas on development. It was also a time when the standards movement was gaining ground across the country and the balanced literacy approach was being introduced in many school districts as a means to improve literacy achievement.

One of the authors participated in a series of Efficacy Seminar workshops in the Bronx, New York. On the first of the 4 days, the participants participated in the ring toss game. The culminating project took place on the fourth day of the seminar. The teachers from the same school developed a goal or project in which they integrated their learnings from the workshops. One group of teachers that the author observed was initially resistant and defensive. The novice teacher in the group inspired them to create a project that incorporated many of the features of reflective practice and constructivism that we have discussed in this chapter. Three Bronx elementary school teachers made up this group:

- Roberta is a veteran Caucasian teacher who is struggling to adapt to the new literacy mandate. She is used to using a basal reader in which stories are incorporated with the phonics approach. In the past, her class library was a reward for those who finished quickly—rarely used in the past few years as school scores plummeted. She is nearing retirement, and until this seminar on personal and child development, she was becoming more and more convinced that the children in her school just could not learn. Roberta stood almost on top of the stand the first time she played the ring toss game.
- Nilda is a second-year bilingual teacher who grew up in the neighborhood as it changed from African American and Puerto Rican to primarily newly arrived immigrants from Mexico, the Dominican Republic, and a host of non-Spanish-speaking countries in Africa and Asia. She studied the balanced literacy approach in college and has been frustrated with the resistance of the more veteran teachers to the approach and with their attitudes toward the children. Nilda stood a little too far away the first time she tossed the rings.
- Mildred has also been teaching for a good number of years. She is African American and believes above all in structure and discipline. She is very wary of an approach that allows kids to choose their own books. "How are little kids going to know what level books to choose?" She blames the home for a lot of the problems the teachers handle on a daily basis. Mildred also stood too close to the stand her first try at the ring toss game.

Roberta: I feel like I've learned a lot about myself and my attitudes toward kids these last three days, but I don't see how that's going to help me develop a curriculum goal or project.

My attitudes may be different, but we've still got to teach the same stuff to the same kids.

Mildred: I see how my changed attitudes can affect my interactions with the kids, but it isn't going to get those parents or guardians to read to their kids or listen to their kids read.

Nilda: I understand your frustrations. But I'm so excited about what I learned about myself from the ring toss game that I want to see how our students could gain from it. Does anyone have any ideas?

(silence ensues)

Roberta: If we could only use the ring toss game with our students in a way that it wouldn't only be a game. If we just do the game, they will get so caught up in it that they won't focus at all on the learning process.

Nilda: What if we related it to something in the curriculum? Maybe something in the balanced literacy program?

Mildred: That's all well and good, but as long as they don't get any backup at home, it's hard to keep up with the mandated pace. Our kids are coming from so far behind that it would be almost impossible to succeed even with parental involvement.

Nilda: Okay. We've got to figure out two things then: how to integrate the ring toss game into our project and maybe literacy curriculum and how to get parents involved.

Roberta: I know where I'm having a lot of trouble and need something to help, or I'm going to give up. I can't get the kids to figure out how to choose books on their own from the class library. Either they choose picture books that are too easy or books they can't read at all.

Mildred: That kind of sounds like the ring toss game. We either were too close or too far away the first time. So if we could somehow get the kids to link the game to their choice of books, that could be a beginning.

Nilda, Roberta, and Mildred continued their brainstorming until they came up with an ingenious plan that allowed their students to understand how to choose the books through the game. In short, the children chose books according to how they played the game the first time—generally, too easy or too hard. When they learned how to apply the ZPD in the game, they then chose their books using the strategies of moderate challenge. Mildred came up with the idea of inviting the parents to an enactment of the ring toss game with their children. The children created their own ring toss game with the help of the art teacher so that they could take it home (especially for the parents or guardians who did not attend). The triumvirate convinced the principal to ask one of the publishers who supplies books for their class libraries to donate books for the event, so that each child took home a book at his or her ZPD.

Reflective Questions

1. What do you think enabled the teachers to use reflective practice here?

2. How is constructivist learning applied at the different levels in this scenario?

3. How could you adapt, apply, or encourage the application of the ZPD in your school?

Chapter Summary

In this chapter, we introduced the dilemmas of standardized testing and high-stakes accountability. We also presented a brief overview of the concepts of reflective practice and constructivist learning that underlie the strategies in the rest of this book. A scenario that demonstrated the intersection of reflective practice and constructivism for adults and students models the multilevel process we advocate. Our conviction that the reflective practice/constructivist model has to be initiated by self-reflective leaders of the school community lies behind the next chapter on leadership styles.

Suggested Readings

Elmore, R. (2003). The problem of stakes in performance-based accountability systems. In S. Fuhrman & R. Elmore (Eds.), *Redesigning accountability systems*. New York: Teachers College Press.

Fosnot, C. (1989). *Enquiring teachers, enquiring learners: A constructivist approach to teaching*. New York: Teachers College Press.

Fosnot, C. T. (1993). *In search of understanding the case for constructivist classrooms*. Alexandria, VA: Association for Supervision and Curriculum Development.

Fullan, M. (1999). *Change forces: The sequel.* Philadelphia: Falmer Press.

Fullan, M. (2003). *Change forces with a vengeance.* London: RoutledgeFalmer.

Herszenhorn, D. M., & Gootman, E. (2004, April 19). City tests loom and third graders feel the heat. *New York Times,* pp. B1, B2.

Lambert, L., Walker, D., Zimmerman, D. P., Cooper, J. E., Lambert, M. D., Gardner, M. E., & Szabo, M. (2003). *The constructivist leader* (2nd ed.). New York: Teachers College Press.

Osterman, K. E., & Kottkamp, R. B. (2004). *Reflective practice for educators: Professional development to improve student learning* (2nd ed.). Thousand Oaks, CA: Corwin.

Piaget, J., & Inhelder, B. (1971). *The psychology of the child.* New York: Basic Books.

Schussler, D. L. (2003). Schools as learning communities: Unpacking the concept. *Journal of School Leadership, 13,* 498–528.

Sergiovanni, T. (1994a). Organizations or communities? Changing the metaphor changes the theory. *Educational Administration Quarterly, 30*(2), 214–226.

Stacey, R. (2001). *Complex responsive processes in organizations.* London: Routledge.

Vygotsky, L. S. (1978). *Mind in society: The development of higher mental process.* Cambridge, MA: Harvard University Press.

Winerip, M. (2004a, April 28). Making leaps but still labeled as failing. *New York Times,* p. B9.

Winerip, M. (2004b, April 4). Principal sees mistake in plan to hold back 3rd graders. *New York Times,* p. B9.

Woolfolk, A., & Hoy, W. K. (2003). *Instructional leadership: A learning-centered guide.* Boston: Allyn & Bacon.

2

Leadership and Self-Knowledge

Leadership is not a personality trait but an attribute of self-development in social relationships.

—Grossman, Wineburg, and Woolworth (2001, p. 996)

Reflective Questions

1. Why is leadership so critical a factor in building and sustaining a learning community?

2. What knowledge, skills, and dispositions do effective leaders possess?

3. Have you seen leaders build and nurture strong communities for learning? Explain.

4. What unique knowledge, skills, and dispositions can you offer as a leader? Be specific and realistic.

Case

Westfield High School (WHS) has been heralded as the first high school in the state to base its curriculum on an inclusionary model.

Teachers in the innovative school are encouraged to develop a deep commitment to inclusion by remaining steadfast in the belief that all children can learn at some developmentally appropriate level. Teachers who possess a critically inclusive predisposition realize that many social and political forces may impinge on their ability to provide high-quality education to all students. Still, these teachers persist and commit to an inclusive educational and pedagogical model. Teachers, leaders in their own right and encouraged by visionary principal "Walter Benjamin" (not real name), developed several competencies for educators who believe in fostering inclusive education. First, they articulated general principles, then ones more specific to inclusion.

The teacher will demonstrate these general principles:

- An awareness to assess factors affecting development and measurement of intelligence in a society comprising dissimilar cultures
- An awareness of learners' value systems, environmental backgrounds, and language patterns
- The need to vary assessment procedures for multicultural differences
- A respect for and acceptance of differences in cultural backgrounds
- An understanding of his or her own prejudices and a commitment to deal with them in interactions with those different from himself or herself

The teacher will demonstrate these specific principles:

- The ability to describe the basic areas of exceptionality and the special needs of exceptional learners
- The ability to perform appropriate screening and diagnostic tests, in conjunction with special education specialists, by objectively observing the behavior and performance of exceptional children
- The expertise to plan, modify, and/or develop instructional materials to identify and instruct learners with exceptionalities
- The ability to remain sensitive to the needs of exceptional learners in the classroom
- The ability to collaborate effectively by respecting the values and opinions of colleagues and primary caregivers

Inclusion is a belief system. It is a process of facilitating an educational environment that provides access to high-quality education for all students (e.g., Kochhar, West, & Taymans, 2000; McLeskey & Waldron, 2001; Wolfendale, 2000). Teachers at WHS believe that all children learning together in the same schools and in the same classrooms, with services and supports necessary so that they can succeed, is critical to a successful school. Maintaining high expectations for all students, believing in their potential, and providing needed services to fully participate are essential components. They believe that no child should be demeaned or have his or her uniqueness ignored or belittled. Students with disabilities should be educated with students without disabilities. Special classes or removal of children from the regular education environment should occur only when the nature or severity of the disability is such that education in the regular classroom cannot be achieved satisfactorily with the use of supplementary support services (Elliott & McKenney, 1998; Morse, 2002).

Walter Benjamin often says that practices that are inclusionary are based on "democratic thought and are a hope for the future." This innovative principal conceived WHS as a learning community in which professional development is not a separate initiative, but rather is built into everything that is done—inclusionary, if you will. He realized that structuring a high school based on inclusionary practice would receive criticism from some parents, students, and community members. "Anything new and forward thinking usually does," he posited to his staff. "We must persist," he proclaimed confidently.

Mr. Benjamin rallied support for his inclusion model over many months at various community forums, at school board meetings, during private encounters, and at the school. He attracted a competent and like-minded staff of professional educators who believed that inclusion was imperative to ensure successful schooling for all students. He demonstrated to parents and students that an inclusionary model would not in any way detract from the educational experiences for students who usually excelled in school. He pointed out that research and his 25 years in education indicated enormous positive benefits of inclusion for all students.

Despite his pep rallies, Mr. Benjamin knew that sound professional development that was initiated from the ground up and was continuous was integral for the success of the program. He initiated a policy-setting body for the school that included administrators, student government representatives, parent association representatives, the union chapter leader, and a representative from each department among the faculty. This group was charged with the responsibility of developing and coordinating professional development activities for two constituencies: parents and community members, and teachers and other educators in the school.

What makes this approach to professional development successful? The answer, Walter Benjamin explained, lies in a variety of factors:

- It is predicated on the belief that leadership is a schoolwide responsibility and that leadership may emerge from any quarter of the school.
- It is built, seamlessly, into the governance and instructional organization of the school.
- It gives teachers the necessary time and decision-making authority to support each other's professional development in and across departments.
- It supports individual professional growth and the sharing of best practices through peer coaching and evaluation by other faculty members, regularly scheduled teacher portfolio presentations, and team-teaching opportunities for faculty members.
- It allows for regular, systematic interaction with the local college and with businesses and community organizations, helping faculty constantly reassess how they are preparing students for higher education and the world of work.
- It shares best practices with the larger educational community through hosting a constant flow of workshops on inclusion as well as showcasing successful efforts in the school.
- It promotes a climate of inquiry and continuous improvement.
- It is driven by a coherent long-term strategy, working backward from graduation requirements to ensure that all students have the necessary supports to meet rigorous graduation criteria.

The role of the principal was critical. His role was aimed at the following:

- Establishing a schoolwide belief that leadership is a shared responsibility
- Establishing a schoolwide belief that the principal represents only a fraction of the leadership necessary for effective schooling
- Establishing a schoolwide belief that everyone has the responsibility to assume some form of leadership
- Establishing a schoolwide focus on teaching and learning
- Building a powerful community of leaders and learners
- Modeling in interactions with teachers the kind of relationships they should develop with students
- Developing a collegial vision and purpose

- Serving as a resource for solving problems and implementing new programs
- Focusing faculty on their own growth and development as well as that of their students
- Evaluating new initiatives in relation to student learning outcomes
- Communicating the mission and philosophy of the school to internal and external audiences
- Enlisting a broad base of political and financial support for ongoing experimentation and innovation

Analysis

Clearly, leadership plays a prominent role in effective schooling. Why else would institutions from all quarters, be they schools, colleges, social agencies, or corporations, place such high regard on securing and remunerating a leader who helps the organization achieve its goals? The literature is replete with studies that document the importance of good leadership (Fullan, 1997; Gardner, 1995; Hansen & Lifton, 1999; *The Jossey-Bass Reader on Educational Leadership*, M. Fullan, Ed., 2000; Patterson, 1993; Sergiovanni, 1996, 2000). Yet leadership means different things to different people, in a variety of settings.

Some individuals still try to adhere to the old industrial leadership (or more accurately, management) model based on an obedient workforce that was predisposed to following orders from above. Others rely on the "one-great-person" theory of leadership. "Hire the right person who will take the bull by its horns and then you'll see profits," one corporate executive confidently proclaimed. Such myopic and restrictive thinking, all too common even in schools, has thwarted effective school practice. A "white knight riding a white horse" mentality remains, regrettably, the metaphor for leadership in too many schools. Certainly, we concur that one person can initiate a bold, forward-looking approach to leadership that is empowering and shared. But to rely on essentially one person to "change the system" is foolhardy and potentially destructive. We all know that schools are too complex for such a provincial view of leadership. Isolated decision making, rule by fiat, and policy mandates have no place in schools structured as learning communities.

Espousing a broader view of leadership within a learning community, you realize the importance of allowing others to assume more responsibility and to participate fully in shared decision making. Since you are a more people-oriented educator, you realize the importance of working closely with other colleagues on instructional, curricular, and administrative matters. Avoiding impersonal or bureaucratic relationships in favor of encouraging personal relationships within a learning community is a worthwhile and necessary leadership goal (Goodlad & McMannon, 1997).

As educational leaders in the 21st century, you realize the enormous challenges you face. As educational leaders, you are prepared to deal with the political, economic, technological, and social realities of schooling. Educational institutions are too complex for the one-person approach to leadership. This chapter supports this broadened view of leadership and the kind of leadership described in the case above, as practiced at WHS.

Democratic schools require stronger leadership than traditional, top-down, autocratic institutions do. The nature of that leadership, however, is markedly different, replacing the need to control with the desire to support. Ironically, such leaders exercise much more influence where it counts, creating dynamic relationships between teachers and students in the classroom and resulting in high standards of academic achievement.

Reflective Questions

1. What conditions are necessary to nurture participative leadership?

2. What is your view of effective leadership?

3. Can everyone lead? Why or why not?

4. Is it really imperative for a leader to possess strong ethical and moral beliefs? Explain.

One question this book addresses is the following: How, in fact, can one model such leadership? How can one build such a learning community, as modeled at WHS, in which leadership is participatory and self-generating, where leadership emerges and is sustained from all quarters? An essential prerequisite for modeling such a learning community is understanding the following premises of leadership:

- *Everyone can lead:* In some way to some degree in a given situation at some time.
- *All leaders are not the same:* Leadership styles, personality, and traits vary greatly.

- *No one way of leading is better than another:* Each leader is talented in a different way.
- *Effective leadership depends on the context:* Matching the right leader to a particular situation is most important.
- *Leadership is relational:* It emerges and develops from a social situation that is nurturing, allowing for trial and error and continuous learning.
- *Effective organizations need all types of leaders:* Different leaders positioned strategically throughout a school or district can contribute greatly to organizational effectiveness.
- *Leadership is, above all else, ethical, and leaders are moral:* Developing ethical and moral leadership is essential for sustaining learning communities.

Chapter Objective

We conceive of leadership as people of different qualities working together toward a shared goal. These people must know their strengths and weaknesses and their personality preferences, and they must also know how they interact with individuals of other quality types. This chapter focuses on self-knowledge as an important attribute of those engaged in activities of leadership. It will encourage and assist you in identifying an appropriate and well-matched style of leadership. Discussion of ethical and moral leadership as related to the quality types will ensue. The chapter concludes with a vignette ("From Theory to Practice") of an administrator who has built this kind of self-knowledge among "leaders" at all levels in her school.

Rationale

Warren Bennis (1989), an authority on leadership, once said that the point is

> not to become a leader. The point is to become yourself, to use yourself completely—all your skills, gifts, and qualities—in order to make your vision manifest. You must withhold nothing. You must, in sum, become the person you started out to be, and enjoy the process of becoming. (pp. 111–112)

This statement summarizes the point of this chapter well. Good leaders know themselves and use their talents to improve schools (see, e.g., Buckingham & Clifton, 2001). Although you are who you are, you can, in Bennis's view, "become": You can grow and improve and become an even better leader.

Moxley (2000), another leadership authority, explained that self-knowledge is

> [an] important attribute of those who engage in the activities of leadership. Our identity helps determine how we understand and practice leadership and engage in relationships that are integral to it. Individuals engaged in the practice of leadership must know their strengths and weaknesses, their personality preferences, what drives and motivates them, and how they have an impact on others. (p. 112)

These are the messages we will amplify in this chapter.

Self-awareness, the ability to form and understand identity, is critical to good leadership. The qualities we possess shape us. They identify who we are and what we can do. Understanding our qualities is the core to understanding ourselves. John Daresh (1996) posited that "knowing oneself" is essential, perhaps even more so than knowing "how to do the job." Aristotle made the point even stronger: "The unexamined life is not worth living."

Leadership has to do with people of different qualities working together toward a shared goal. Leadership does not focus solely on the capacity of one person, usually called the "boss." Although a "boss" is the staple of most organizations, other individuals with different characteristics or qualities are equally essential. Leadership in this sense is a broad, inclusive activity in which combinations of quality groups work together toward a common goal.

Working together toward a common goal presupposes that we have identified the right individual for a particular task or situation. Good leaders ask, "Do we need an architect? An innovator? A stabilizer? A campaigner? A healer? A designer? A sustainer?" How we match the leadership quality (style, character, personality) of an individual to the needs of the situation is critical for effective leadership.

Leadership Qualities

Assessing Your Leadership Style: The Survey

The ideas in this section are drawn from Glanz (2002; based on Null, 1996) but have been extended and refined based on ensuing research. Complete the following survey, meant to provide feedback to explore your leadership proclivities.

Directions for Completing the Survey*

1. Below, you will find fifty-six (56) statements.

2. Next to each number, write True (T) or False (F) for each statement.

3. If a statement describes the way you think you are, for the most part, then indicate True (T); if the statement does not describe you, indicate False (F). You MUST write True (T) or False (F). Some statements may be difficult to classify, but please indicate just one answer.

4. Your responses are anonymous. The surveys cannot accurately assess these attributes without your forthright responses to the various statements. You need not share your responses with anyone. Obviously, the accuracy of these instruments is dependent both on the truthfulness of your responses and the degree to which you are aware that you possess or lack a certain attribute.

5. Using the chart below, circle numbers that you recorded as true.

6. After you complete the survey by recording your responses in the chart below, follow the directions to tabulate and interpret the results on page 36.

Answer Sheet (Answer True or False to Each Statement in Each Survey)

Am I an AAS?	Am I a CAS?	Am I an AS?	Am I a DAS?	Am I a DS?	Am I a DAG?	Am I an AAG?
1	2	3	4	5	6	7
14	13	12	11	10	9	8
16	15	18	17	20	19	21
30	29	22	24	23	28	25
31	39	32	27	26	41	33
35	40	36	37	34	47	42
38	44	46	48	45	49	43
56	55	50	54	51	53	52

*SOURCE: From *Who Are You, Really? Understanding Your Life's Energy* by Gary Null. Copyright © 1996. New York: Carroll & Graf, a division of Avalon Publishing Group. Used with permission.

The Survey

1. I feel I'm good at supervising a small group of people, and I enjoy doing so.

2. When I'm in a new situation, such as a new job setting or relationship, I spend a lot of time comparing it to analogous situations I've been in previously.

3. I believe that respect for authority is one of the cornerstones of good character.

4. I enjoy thinking about large issues, such as how society is organized politically.

5. I get asked for help a lot, and have a hard time saying no.

6. Ever since childhood, I've always seemed to want more out of life than my peers did.

7. When I first enter a new environment, such as a workplace or a school, I make it a point to become acquainted with as many people as possible.

8. I rarely seek quiet.

9. I can work harder than most people, and I enjoy doing so.

10. When I meet a person, I'll give that individual the benefit of the doubt; in other words, I'll like him until he gives me a reason not to.

11. The idea of a lifelong and exclusive intimate partner doesn't seem desirable or realistic for me.

12. A lifelong relationship with a romantic partner is one of my goals.

13. I can sometimes work creatively at full throttle for hours on end and not notice the passage of time.

14. I believe that divorce is to be strongly avoided whenever possible.

15. I'll periodically go through extremely low-energy periods during which I have to remind myself that it is only a phase.

16. When it comes to spending and saving habits, I take pride in being more thrifty and less foolish than most people.

17. Being alone does not scare me; in fact, I do some of my best thinking when I'm alone.

18. My extended family is the most important part of my social life.

19. I spend much less time than others do on what I consider pointless leisure pursuits, such as TV and movie watching; novel reading; and card, computer, or board game playing.

20. I procrastinate a lot.

21. My vacations are always highly structured; several days of just sitting in one place and vegetating would drive me crazy.

22. Directing a big job and supervising a lot of subordinates is my idea of a headache.

23. People usually like me.

24. I find myself getting frustrated because most people's world-views are so limited.

25. Networking as a career and life tool is something that comes naturally to me.

26. I'm happiest interacting with people and aiding them in some way.

27. I have a drive to express my ideas and influence the thinking of others.

28. I find myself getting frustrated because most people operate at a slower pace than I do.

29. I find myself getting frustrated because most people are not on my mental wavelength.

30. I generally believe that if individuals behave outside the norms of society, they should be prepared to pay the price.

31. My home is more organized and cleaner than most people's in my neighborhood.

32. Holding one job for decades would be okay with me if the conditions were good and the boss were nice.

33. When tackling a problem or task, I'm usually less defeatist than others.

34. It sometimes takes an outside force to get me motivated because I tend to be satisfied with what I have.

35. I enjoy the feeling of my life going along at an even pace like a well-oiled machine; too many stops and starts and ups and downs would really upset me.

36. Trying to lengthen your life by eating the "right" foods doesn't make much sense to me because when your time's up, your time's up.

37. I have no trouble getting people to listen to me and grasp what I'm saying.

38. I understand that detail work is what ultimately gets a job done, and I have the gumption and know-how to tackle details.

39. Working by myself is no problem; in fact, I prefer it.

40. At times, ideas just "come to me," and if I can't put them down then and there on paper, canvas, etc., I'll be uncomfortable until I can.

41. I could never be really happy working for someone else.

42. I like associating with influential people and am not intimidated by them.

43. I'm happiest moving and doing, as opposed to sitting and thinking.

44. Throughout my life, there's been a pattern of people calling me one or more of the following: "temperamental," "moody," "sad," "flighty," "different"; and I never really felt like I was "one of the boys/girls."

45. People tell me I have a great sense of humor.

46. I believe that blood is thicker than water and that it is more important to be loyal to your relatives than to your friends.

47. I don't have much time or patience for long family gatherings, such as a whole afternoon spent celebrating Thanksgiving.

48. The makeup of my social circle is constantly changing.

49. Managing a big job and having subordinates carry out the detail work is my ideal kind of endeavor.

50. I prefer to work at a job a set number of hours each day and then have the rest of the 24 hours for relaxation.

51. I'm good at smoothing over others' conflicts and helping to mediate them.

52. I thrive on setting goals for myself and then figuring out how to reach them; I can't imagine just drifting through life without a plan.

53. I'm more intelligent than most people, and others almost always recognize this.

54. I can't fathom the idea of holding one job for decades.

55. I find competition distasteful.

56. I would never dress in a flashy, bohemian, or otherwise attention-getting way.

Directions for Tabulating the Results

1. For each category (e.g., "Am I an AAS?") count the number of True (T) responses in that column. Record your fraction score on the chart below. Note that the numerator represents the number of "True" responses and the denominator represents the total number of questions on the survey (which will always equal eight because each survey has eight questions). For example, if you recorded "T" for seven out of the eight items in the first column, "Am I an AAS?" then your fraction will be 7/8.

2. Complete the table below by referring to your responses on the Answer Sheet on page 32.

	Am I an AAS?	Am I a CAS?	Am I an AS?	Am I a DAS?	Am I a DS?	Am I a DAG?	Am I an AAG?
T's/8							

Interpreting the Results

1. Your "Natural Leadership Quality" is found under the category in which you scored the highest number of "True" responses. For example, if you scored 8/8 for "Am I a DS?" then your quality is "DS." (For a description of qualities, see "Assessing Your Leadership Style: What It Means" below.) Perhaps no category earned an 8/8, but one category (e.g.,

"Am I a CAS?") had 7/8, whereas all the others were lower (6/8 and less). In that case, your quality is "CAS."

2. Although most respondents will find their highest score in one category, some respondents may have two or more categories with the highest scores. For example, you may have scored an 8/8 in two categories. If so, then your quality is represented by those two categories. If no category received an 8/8, locate the next-highest score. For example, your highest score may be 5/8, and three categories may have earned that score. If this is the case, then your quality is represented by those three categories.

3. In the chart below, circle the quality or qualities that scored the highest "True" responses.

AAS	CAS	AS	DAS	DS	DAG	AAG

4. The meaning of these results will become clear as you read the remainder of this chapter. Please note the following caution: No one assessment can accurately assess one's inclinations or abilities. These surveys are meant to stimulate interest, thought, and discussion for purposes of exploring leadership in schools. Examine the results in light of the theories and ideas expressed in this book, and make your own determination of their relevance and applicability to you personally and to your work in schools.

Assessing Your Leadership Style: What It Means

Each of us manifests a particular quality or style. We feel most comfortable when we exercise discretion to use and live by that style. The qualities are as follows:

- Dynamic Aggressives (DAG)   Represent the smallest percentage of the population
- Dynamic Assertives (DAS)   Represent the change agents, reformers, or iconoclasts
- Dynamic Supportives (DS)   Represent the nurturing helpers
- Adaptive Aggressives (AAG) Represent individuals who aggressively pursue a goal
- Adaptive Assertives (AAS)   Represent excellent organizers

- Adaptive Supportives (AS)   Represent most of the people
                                  one ever meets
- Creative Assertives (CAS)   Represent visionary and artistic
                                  individuals

We will next examine each of these qualities by defining its essential characteristics and how each quality manifests itself in different people.

We have natural qualities and attributes that make us unique and that drive or motivate us. How we react in a particular situation or crisis is determined by these "natural" qualities. While many of us possess a constellation of attributes in differing amounts, we fall back on that dominant attribute or personality trait that comes most "naturally" to us in times of crisis or need.

A superintendent, for example, may have been hired in a district that has been beset by "warring" factions to articulate a community vision in which all vested interests can reach consensus. Yet this superintendent, although managerially very competent, may not have the "natural" dynamic and charismatic qualities to bridge disparate viewpoints and factions. We must consider the match between the "natural quality" and the task that needs to be accomplished. Not everyone has the same potential to bring the aforementioned district to consensus. The superintendent, while competent and able to do many important things, may not be a good match for the needs of this district at this time.

What can we say about these attributes or qualities in general? On one end of the spectrum, an individual may demonstrate charisma that can naturally influence or attract other people. On the other end of the quality spectrum are people who have no need to stand out in any way. Rather, their expertise is in their ability to adapt well to any situation and to work diligently to accomplish their objectives. Each of these qualities, and the ones in between, has its own resonance, strengths, and weaknesses.

The Primary Quality Types

Three main types of people in terms of their natural leadership quality exist: the Dynamics, the Adaptives, and the Creatives (see Figure 2.1). Dynamic individuals possess a charismatic quality, a personal magnetism that enables them to inspire and lead others. Dynamics have an ability to see the larger picture, can articulate a vision for the future, and have a strong sense of ego (think of

Figure 2.1   Primary Quality Types

- Dynamics – Would others characterize you as highly charismatic?
- Adaptives – Would others realize that although you are neither charismatic nor creative, you adapt well to varied situations?
- Creatives – Would others acknowledge your imaginative or artistic ability?

Margaret Thatcher, Bill Clinton, or Nelson Mandela as examples of this primary quality type). Adaptives, in contrast, are not charismatic nor are they looking to change the broad scope of situations; their sense of ego is much less than Dynamics'. Creatives have a different personal rhythm, awareness, and sensitivity that allow them to perceive the world differently and more imaginatively than Dynamics or Adaptives.

These three main quality types are distinct from one another. If you've met a Dynamic individual, you are not likely to forget him or her. They take center stage and possess the personal magnetism that attracts others to them and their ideas. These qualities occur "naturally." An Adaptive or Creative, in contrast, may "act" or appear charismatic at times, but this characteristic doesn't come naturally. The characteristics of each quality occur naturally and without contrivance.

The Secondary Quality Types

Within the broad types, three further divisions exist. Some people are characteristically aggressive, some assertive, and some supportive (see Figure 2.2).

Figure 2.2   Secondary Quality Types

- Aggressives – Would others characterize you as highly opinionated or even contentious?
- Assertives – Would others realize that you are a secure and confident person?
- Supportives – Would others acknowledge your encouraging and affable nature?

The Aggressives have a driving, forceful quality and tend to lead or want to dominate others. These are dominating, take-charge people. Have you ever served on a committee and noticed one individual who immediately engages the group forcefully? These individuals have a need to be center stage.

In contrast, some people feel quite comfortable to sit back and listen. Although these people, the Assertives, are not driven to take charge immediately, they are confident and will be willing to put forth their strong views on matters at the right moment.

Supportive individuals are not the natural leaders, and they are not usually the most eloquent speakers. They act best in their supportive roles. They are basically nurturing, happy to help, and truly concerned about the welfare of others.

Putting Them Together to Form Seven Quality Types

All of us, of course, possess a degree of each quality. We all can demonstrate, at times, creativity, assertiveness, and even dynamism. Again, the point is that each of us has a "predominant" natural quality. When we operate in our quality types, we feel most comfortable and productive. It is "who we really are" when the curtains are drawn and we are alone.

As noted above, the primary qualities combine with the secondary qualities to form seven distinct quality types (see Figure 2.3). For a complete discussion of each of the seven quality types, see Glanz (2002). Research data confirm the principles below:

- Most people exhibit a tendency toward one quality over another. In cases where individuals exhibit strong tendencies in more than one area, the qualities are likely complementary.
- We exhibit particular qualities as a natural consequence of who we are. In other words, these qualities manifest themselves uniquely and naturally. The particular quality comes easily and automatically to us. For instance, I may act dynamically, but if I am not naturally dynamic, I may come off as just plain pushy. Each person should be allowed to express himself or herself in a specific quality. For example, parents who both are Creative Assertives may have a child who naturally displays Adaptive Assertive tendencies. If these parents "coerce" the child to behave in a certain way based on their own qualities, the child will likely feel upset and dysfunctional. An Adaptive Assertive child can never display the natural creativeness that Creative Assertives manifest.

Each quality operates on a high (up) and low (down) end and in between. A Dynamic Aggressive, for instance, may work to his or her potential and thereby achieve much good for an organization. If,

Figure 2.3   Seven Quality Types

	D	A	C
AG	DAG (Dynamic Aggressive)	AAG (Adaptive Aggressive)	
AS	DAS (Dynamic Assertive)	AAS (Adaptive Assertive)	CAS (Creative Assertive)
S	DS (Dynamic Supportive)	AS (Adaptive Supportive)	

however, the person is operating at the low end, he or she may exhibit some rather obnoxious and unethical behaviors and thus not contribute very much to the organization. In fact, operating at the low end of the Dynamic Aggressive quality may cause the most harm to an organization.

Reflective Questions

1. Assess your personal leadership style. What did you learn or confirm about yourself?

2. How can these leadership styles help build effective learning communities?

3. Have your views of leadership changed in any way? Why or why not?

Conclusions About Leadership Qualities

School systems are too complex for leadership to be reserved for the select few. Although school systems may need the "head" leadership of a Dynamic Aggressive, they need a full complement of educators serving in different capacities to effect the overall desired systemic changes. School systems need the overarching insight of a Dynamic Assertive to jump-start whole school reform. They also need the personal charisma of a Dynamic Supportive, the steadfastness of an Adaptive Aggressive, the organizational skills of an Adaptive Assertive, the devotion to sound values of an Adaptive Supportive, and the creative problem-solving ability of a Creative Assertive. The point is that different individuals exemplify these character qualities and that all people should be encouraged to share their unique talents for the improvement of schools or districts.

Practicing Ethical and Moral Leadership

Effective leaders build integrity and character through their work. To paraphrase Peter Drucker (1999), good leaders lead not through the knowledge and skills, but through responsibility and integrity (p. 2). Ethical and moral leadership is an imperative in building effective and sustaining learning communities (Sergiovanni, 1992; Starratt, 2003). Without an ethical and moral stance, a leader, regardless of the quality type, will lead perfunctorily, without "soul" (Bolman & Deal, 2002). Much has been written about ethical and moral leadership (e.g., Maxcy, 2002). In this section of the chapter, we will underscore the importance of this and indicate briefly how ethical and moral leadership intersects with the leadership qualities as described previously in the chapter. As you read the information that follows, think how you might best actualize your own ethical and moral behavior as leaders by avoiding some natural negative tendencies and always striving for an ideal.

Ethics deals with actions that are commonly seen as right or wrong. Showing favoritism to a colleague who is white over someone who is black in terms of hiring is prejudicial and discriminatory; it is simply wrongheaded. An ethical leader strives to do things right as well as do the right things. Morality deals with a system of values that undergirds ethical behavior. A moral leader might value social justice and equity for all people. If his or her behavior is consistent, then he or she will act "morally" when the particular value is necessary in a given situation. Since the leader values social justice, he or she will consciously remain on guard for possible prejudicial behavior in selecting a new hire.

Ethical and moral dilemmas are very commonplace. The situation is not always black and white, excuse the expression. How you as a leader draw upon your proclivities and sensitivities toward ethical and moral behavior will determine the extent to which you are effective in building and sustaining a learning community.

Dynamic and Adaptive Aggressives have the strongest tendencies, among all the quality types, to act in less-than-ethical ways. Because they are so goal oriented, they sometimes, especially working at the lower end of their potential continuum, will state that "the ends justify the means." Dynamic Aggressives simply might not care that their actions hurt others as long as their needs are satisfied or goals accomplished. Adaptive Aggressives are always conniving, dealing, and moving to accomplish their agenda. In their haste, they tend not to sit back and reflect upon the consequences of their actions.

Adaptive Supportives and Creative Assertives would rarely claim that the ends justify the means. They are not as goal driven and compulsive as other quality types and would rarely resort to unethical, immoral behavior to achieve an end. Dynamic and Adaptive Assertives fall somewhere in the middle. They too, like Dynamic and Adaptive Aggressives, are goal driven and might at times be easily swayed toward unethical conduct. They might cleverly rationalize their actions without fully comprehending the consequences of their behavior. They must be constantly vigilant to remain aware of their proclivities.

Dynamic Supportives, and our guess is that many readers of this chapter fall into this quality category, are caring, sensitive leaders who try their utmost to help others, sometimes at their own expense. They too, like Adaptive Supportives and Creative Assertives, have a strong system of values that nurture ethical and moral conduct. However, unlike them, they have a tendency when under stress to succumb to unethical practices.

These aforementioned categorizations are obviously generalizations, and no one individual should be stigmatized as unethical and immoral. Our point here, as it is in this chapter, is that we are human and we have human potentialities and leadership proclivities. Such qualities make us who we are, make us unique. We are all bombarded by dilemmas that challenge our moral and ethical sensitivities. The extent to which we act ethically and morally depends on who we are (quality type)—but most important, on how aware we remain of our ethical and moral obligations as leaders.

Reflective Class Practice

At this point, pair off with a colleague and construct possible responses to the following three scenarios:

1. Identify two dilemmas that might entail a difficult moral/ethical leadership issue; using your leadership style, discuss how each of you might approach the situation.

(Continued)

(Continued)

2. You are a principal of a newly built school, and you desire to create a "textbook" learning community. Discuss steps you would take to initiate such a community (define terms and state objectives).

3. How might you adapt the vision and practices of WHS, as described at the outset of the chapter, in your school or district?

From Theory to Practice

"Sandra Braithwaite" is superintendent of a large inner-city school district that has nearly 11,000 students in Grades K–12. She is a take-charge, visionary leader (a Dynamic Assertive, of course) who has recently been appointed to "revitalize" the district. Charged by the school board specifically to improve reading and math scores and raise achievement levels across the curriculum, the new district superintendent, conversant with current literature in the field, decides to put together a leadership team to spearhead reform efforts in the district. Dr. Braithwaite's goal is to build a learning community by developing and nurturing connections between people, socially and intellectually. At a staff meeting, she explains, "Building a learning community is tantamount to developing a commitment to shared learning." Dr. Braithwaite realizes that the only way to eventually raise student achievement is to focus on instructional leadership. She realizes she needs to appoint individuals to principalships and assistant principalships who have a strong commitment to instructional improvement. Past practices in the district, however, have relied on hiring supervisors who are good managers but not necessarily effective instructional leaders. She realizes that emerging trends in supervisory practice must emphasize (a) training for administrators as well as teachers in supervision, mentoring, and coaching; (b) sensitivity to the processes of professional growth and continuous improvement; (c) training in observation and reflection on practice; (d) integration of supervision with staff development, curriculum development, and school improvement systems; and (e) collegial assistance among educators, parents, and students, and so on. In sum, she wants leaders who believe that supervision of instruction must be collaborative, collegial, and democratic.

While Dr. Braithwaite is conversant with the literature on instructional improvement, she is equally conversant in the theories of natural leadership qualities. Having read this chapter, taken the surveys, and understood the interrelationships among qualities and the importance of ethical and moral leadership, she is now ready to put these ideas into action. She knows that many educators may have the requisite knowledge and skills to enhance instructional leadership. But she asks, "Are they in the right positions to be able to transform knowledge into action?" She understands that espousing a democratic and collaborative vision is very different from making it a reality. She also realizes the political dimension required in transforming a school or a district. She wants leaders who not only understand this political dimension but also have the gumption (courage and imagination) to make the tough decisions that would be required.

Dr. Braithwaite has been given authority to appoint not only a cadre of leaders in the district office but also individuals in interim principalships. She has a list of two dozen candidates who have reputations as strong instructional leaders with proven records of performance. Yet she realizes that leadership is situational. An effective principal in one setting (e.g., an affluent neighborhood with multiple resources and a majority of untenured teachers) may be less so in another (e.g., an inner-city neighborhood with fewer resources and a majority of tenured teachers). Braithwaite begins to match individual strengths with situational requirements. Although certainly not an exact science, such an undertaking is guided by several key questions that she poses:

- What are the position vacancies (i.e., principal vacancies and positions in the district office)?
- What are the unique needs of each school (considering demographics, experience levels of teachers, achievement scores, current instructional programs, PTA membership, etc.)? What kind of team will she need in the district office to carry out her new instructional policies?
- What are the specific challenges in each school (e.g., is the school in disarray organizationally, does the school lack visionary leadership, or are teachers complacent and lack the motivation to try harder)? What is the "heart" of the problem that exists in a particular school?
- What are the unique strengths of each (principal and district leader) candidate?

Dr. Braithwaite identifies characteristics she deems necessary for each school. She makes a grid that identifies each school and lists three major requirements that would make it more effective. For example, School X has a sound curriculum, sufficient instructional materials, and adequate "person power" but lacks a leader who can empower other leaders to form a learning community. She then lists each principal candidate and lists each one's major quality. School X, according to Braithwaite, needs a Dynamic Assertive leader who can rock the boat and motivate the many participants to a collective vision. The candidate must demonstrate, above all else, a strong system of values that encourages ethical behavior. No matter how qualified Candidate X is with his years of excellent service and outstanding organizational skills, without a value system that supports ethical conduct, he would be the wrong leader in this particular school. As an Adaptive Assertive, he would be better suited in School Y, which needs someone who can coordinate and organize instructional activities in a more coherent fashion than has been done in the past.

As for her team in the district office, Dr. Braithwaite establishes goals and objectives for each position and then matches the qualities to the position. For example, she wants a team member or two who are expert instructional leaders and can relate to teachers in a nonauthoritarian manner. She may decide, then, to select a Dynamic Supportive or even an Adaptive Supportive individual to fill these positions. On the other hand, she will need an individual to wade through the politics and oppositions that inevitably arise in every change effort. Therefore she knows she needs an Adaptive Aggressive who will ensure, at all costs, that the vision becomes a reality.

Above all, Dr. Braithwaite knows that she wants leaders, not followers. She wants to empower her leadership team so that they, in turn, will empower others. Developing a learning community where individual strengths of all educators are identified, valued, and nurtured is central to her task. Effective leadership, for Dr. Braithwaite, relies on individuals of different qualities working together toward a shared goal.

Reflective Site Implementation

Discuss the steps you would take in your school/district to implement a learning community similar to the one that Dr. Braithwaite was developing in the case above. What challenges/obstacles would you likely face, and how might you begin to overcome them?

Suggested Readings

Fullan, M. (Ed.). (2000). *The Jossey-Bass reader on educational leadership.* San Francisco: Jossey-Bass.

Glanz, J. (2002). *Finding your leadership style: A guide for educators.* Alexandria, VA: Association for Supervision and Curriculum Development.

Maxcy, S. J. (2002). *Ethical school leadership.* Lanham, MD: Scarecrow.

Patterson, J. L. (1993). *Leadership for tomorrow's schools.* Alexandria, VA: Association for Supervision and Curriculum Development.

Sergiovanni, T. J. (1996). *Leadership for the schoolhouse: How is it different? Why is it important?* San Francisco: Jossey-Bass.

3

Let Us Learn

Ruth Powers Silverberg

Learning about learning is not for the fainthearted educator who does not possess the resolve to make a difference. Learning about learning will not allow a teacher, a school leader, or an educator to simply maintain the status quo of the classroom—although many voices, including those of academics, politicians, and parents, call for relief on behalf of the learner, as practitioners, we are in a position to do something about it.

—Johnston (1996, p. 206)

Reflective Questions

1. Where do you learn best?

2. What do you do well (or particularly enjoy doing)?

3. How did you learn to do it?

4. How would you teach someone to do the thing you just described?

Learning is the core technology of schooling. Students learn in classrooms, teachers and administrators learn from each other and their students and in professional development (we hope), and parents and other community members learn in PTA and other meetings. While this may sound obvious, your answers to the questions above may highlight the gap that often exists between learning and schooling. We propose the possibility of closing that gap.

Most people, when asked to identify the core technology (work) of schooling, say "teaching." But teaching has not occurred if learning has not occurred; teaching and learning are interactive processes. Learning does not require a teacher, but teaching requires a learner. Without learning, we can safely say that teaching—however well planned and "delivered," based upon standards and sound pedagogical theory—has not taken place.

The goal of this chapter is to present a process through which the whole school community can focus on learning, and more important, learners, so that EVERYONE can learn what he or she needs to learn to have a rewarding, productive life.

First Things First: What Is Learning, and How Does It Occur?

Throughout this book, learning is defined as the construction of meaning from experience. Learning is NOT "delivered" by one person to another. Meaning construction, when facilitated by another person, whether it is a formal teacher or a peer, is most likely to occur in a *relational space.* This relational space is created through shared understanding and mutual recognition. Simply put, individuals need to be fully engaged for meaning construction to occur, and full engagement requires the learner to bring all of his or her abilities and experiences to the learning process. We have all observed that learners whose experiences or ways of thinking are marginalized in the learning situation are less likely to learn; this is why we work so hard to create learning experiences that are culturally and cognitively inclusive. But the relational space depends on *shared, mutual recognition*—not recognition of one person by the other, but recognition by both parties of themselves and the other. This requires an understanding and ability to articulate and communicate our ways of processing our experience. Again, learning and teaching are interactive processes. We make meaning together when we "put our minds together" and create new understandings of the world.

So How Do I "Understand," Articulate, and Communicate How I Learn?

Step 1 in the development of relational space is an understanding of myself. As teachers, some of us may have performed some activities designed to develop awareness of our ways of learning during our teacher preparation or professional development. However, this experience too often does not take place. Teacher development programs tend to focus on understanding the students, becoming an expert diagnostician. The teacher himself or herself is not considered a worthy focus in improvement of instruction. This phenomenon is peculiar, especially given that we know that the largest influences on how teachers teach are their own past teachers and experiences as students. All of the pedagogical theory and child psychology take a backseat to internalized experience in moments of stress—and teaching is stressful.

There are many approaches to developing greater awareness of our internalized drivers, some of which are explored in this book. This chapter presents an approach to developing awareness of self and other as learners, the "Let Me Learn" Process (LMLP). Through extensive, personal reflective work and application of the findings of the Learning Connections Inventory (LCI), students, teachers, and administrators can understand, articulate, and communicate their distinctive ways of processing the world. This understanding creates the foundation for a community of learners, working together in a relational space.

The "Let Me Learn" Process[1]

The theoretical foundation of the Let Me Learn Process (LMLP) is the Interactive Learning Model (ILM), developed by Johnston (1996, 1998, 2004a, 2004b, 2005) and refined over the last 10 years through applications of empirical evidence of its effects. The ILM depicts three interactive processes of learning—cognition (thinking), affectation (feeling), and conation (doing)—as the mesh through which the brain/mind interface occurs. Each of these three processes is revealed as a unique combination of four learning patterns: sequence, precision, technical reasoning, and confluence. These patterns are defined as follows:

Sequence: The process of organizing and planning; seeking order and consistency

Precision: The process of using information and words; detail-oriented, seeking confirmation of what is valid, right, and/or true

Technical reasoning:	The process of hands-on, active, autonomous problem solving; seeks real-world relevance and the time and space to figure things out
Confluence:	The process of generating ideas, reading between the lines, and making connections; comfortable with taking risks, trying and failing and trying again; seeking to do it "my own way"

The four patterns work interactively as a team to form the internal voice of our metacognition. Key to who we are as learners is how these processes interface with the working memory of the mind, helping to translate the neuro-impulses of the brain into symbolic representation (language, numbers, musical notes, etc.), which the mind stores and retrieves as needed.

Teachers learn to use the ILM in a LMLP inservice workshop or graduate course. The LMLP is an approach to teaching and learning that provides students and teachers with the tools to identify their unique learning patterns and the tools to use this knowledge with intention (Johnston, 1996, 1998). It also provides a framework and vocabulary that allow all members of the school community to communicate about their central concern, learning—learning for students, learning for teachers, and learning for families.

More About the Learning Connections Inventory

The LCI is a 28-item self-report survey instrument developed and tested for reliability and validity over a period of 3 years by Christine Johnston and Gary Dainton to capture each learner's distinct combination of the four learning patterns: sequence, precision, technical reasoning, and confluence.[2] The LCI is available in seven versions for use in education, work, and family settings. Its widespread use in schools and corporations throughout the world continues to contribute to the validation and growth of the instrument and the LMLP. The instrument is *not* a test or a diagnostic or assessment tool. It is simply a vehicle through which each learner can communicate his or her natural learning processes.

The inventory consists of 28 items requiring the learner to respond by circling "never ever," "almost never," "sometimes," "almost always," or "always." The two sample items appearing at the beginning of the Professional Form are reprinted here for clarification.

A. I listen carefully whenever directions are given.

NEVER EVER   ALMOST NEVER   SOMETIMES   ALMOST ALWAYS   ALWAYS

B. I like to show my knowledge by giving impromptu presentations.

NEVER EVER   ALMOST NEVER   SOMETIMES   ALMOST ALWAYS   ALWAYS

Item "A" codes in the sequential process, and Item "B" codes in the confluent process. The following are items from the LCI code in the precise and technical processes, respectively.

I pride myself in giving factually correct answers to the questions I am asked.

NEVER EVER   ALMOST NEVER   SOMETIMES   ALMOST ALWAYS   ALWAYS

I like to take things apart to see how they work.

NEVER EVER   ALMOST NEVER   SOMETIMES   ALMOST ALWAYS   ALWAYS

The inventory ends with three short-answer items used to validate the scale scores, which are tabulated on the last page. The validation process requires facility with the conceptual bases of the ILM and the LMLP, and it is most accurately completed by someone who has taken a course or workshop in the process *and* has experience using the process. The scores indicate the individual's learning patterns, or unique combination of the four processes the learner has a drive to "use first," "use as needed," or "avoid." For example, scale scores of Sequential Process: 32; Precise Process: 22; Technical Process: 15; and Confluent Process: 20 indicate that the learner engages in a learning activity by first using the sequential process (looking for step-by-step directions, feeling satisfied only when the task is complete, double-checking the final product), avoiding the technical process (working alone to complete the task by diving in and doing it), and using the precise process and confluent process as needed.

The most distinctive quality of Let Me Learn, which distinguishes it from "learning style" approaches, is that the students *and* the teacher take the LCI, so information about the students' and teacher's learning is collected and shared by all members of the class. This process gives everyone a shared understanding and vocabulary for communicating about his or her own and each other's thoughts, feelings, and actions. The theory-in-use supporting the LMLP is this: Everyone learns, and our distinctive ways of learning can be understood by ourselves and each other, using tools for data collection including the LCI. Through our understanding, we can create a relational space where we construct meaning from experience together, leading to a truly shared vision for learning and schooling.

The Process at Work

Teachers and the Let Me Learn Process

Teachers are typically the first to experience the LMLP in a school district. While there are a variety of ways to introduce the process, the usual method is an "awareness workshop" given for an entire faculty or group of teachers from one level or one school. The workshop is $1\frac{1}{2}$ to 2 hours long. It includes activities to help the participants use data about themselves and their own learning and schooling in order to begin to understand the framework and vocabulary of the LMLP.

A typical first activity asks participants to draw a picture of "where they learn best." After encouragement to "think outside the box," teachers rarely draw a classroom. Some draw a picture of their living room, some of the beach, and some of places where they learned their favorite hobby, such as a gym. Sharing of pictures leads to the conclusion that learning and schooling are not necessarily the same thing and that learning is happening for everyone everywhere. One or two teachers invariably state the realization that their students learn outside of the classroom as well as inside. To focus on the three parts of the ILM, participants use a piece of paper divided in thirds to depict what they are thinking, feeling, and doing during an activity they do well. The ways participants choose to do the activity vary and provide more data about the individual's learning patterns; some participants write extensive descriptions, some write a word or phrase, and others draw a picture, using no words at all. Again, the products are shared and discussed. These activities make learning (not schooling or "teaching") the focus of the work, with the ILM serving as the lens.

The facilitator then provides a brief introduction to the LCI, and each participant completes and scores his or her own inventory. Facilitators validate the scores as much as possible depending on the size of the group, and the teachers are then introduced to the vocabulary of the patterns in Table 3.1 and Table 3.2. Table 3.1 describes how a pattern is likely to present itself if it is used first; Table 3.2 describes what happens if the pattern is avoided.

When participants see themselves in the chart and hear their own internal voices saying the phrases in the last column (some find the exact words they wrote on the short-answer section of LCI), they begin to understand the power of the LCI to capture unique approaches to learning.

Teachers interested in pursuing greater understanding of the process then sign up for the full implementation, which consists of monthly sessions throughout the school year, facilitated by a certified

Table 3.1   Learning Pattern Characteristics

	How I think	*How I do things*	*How I feel*	*What I might say*
Sequential	I organize information I mentally analyze data I break tasks down into steps	I make lists I organize I plan first, *then* act	I thrive on consistency and dependability I need things to be tidy and organized I feel frustrated when the game plan keeps changing I feel frustrated when I'm rushed	Could I see an example? I need more time to double-check my work Could we review those directions? A place for everything and everything in its place What are my priorities?
Precise	I research information I ask *lots* of questions I always want to know more	I challenge statements and ideas that I doubt I prove I am right I document my research and findings I write things down I write long e-mail messages and leave long voicemail messages	I thrive on knowledge I feel good when I am correct I feel frustrated when incorrect information is accepted as valid I feel frustrated when people do not share information with me	I need more information Let me write up the answer to that Can we play trivia? I'm currently reading three different books Did you get my e-mail on that? Did you know that . . . Actually . . .

(Continued)

LML consultant. Consultants are not only well versed in use of the process, they have also been intensively educated in using the process as the central tool for their own reflective practice.

Table 3.1 (Continued)

	How I think	*How I do things*	*How I feel*	*What I might say*
Technical	I seek concrete relevance— what does this mean in the real world? I only want as much information as I need— nothing extraneous	I get my hands on I tinker I solve the problem I *do*	I enjoy knowing how things work I feel good that I am self-sufficient I feel frustrated when the task has no real-world relevance I enjoy knowing things, but I do not feel the need to share that knowledge	I can do it myself Let me show you how . . . I don't want to read a book about it, I want to *do* it How will I ever use this in the real world? How can I *fix* this? I could use a little space . . .
Confluent	I read between the lines I think outside the box I brainstorm I make obscure connections between things that are seemingly unrelated	I take risks I am not afraid to fail I talk about things—a lot I might start things and not finish them I will start a task first— *then* ask for directions	I enjoy energy I feel comfortable with failure I do not enjoy having my ideas criticized I feel frustrated by people who are not open to new ideas I enjoy a challenge I feel frustrated by repeating a task over and over	What do you mean, "that's the way we've always done it"?! The rules don't apply to me Let me tell you about . . . I have an idea . . . I have another idea . . .

SOURCE: Used with permission of Let Me Learn, Inc., Center for Advancement of Learning.

Consultants understand how their own learning patterns influence their facilitation and how the patterns of each group's participants inform the way the learning will occur. As a result, the workshop is

Table 3.2   When I Avoid a Pattern

	How I think	*How I do things*	*How I feel*	*What I might say*
Sequential	These directions make no sense! I did this before—why repeat it? Why can't I just jump in?	Avoid direction; avoid practice Can't get the pieces in order Ignore table of contents, indexes, and syllabi Leave the task incomplete	Jumbled Scattered Out of sync Untethered Unfettered Unanchored	Do I have to do it again? Why do I have to follow directions? Does it matter what we do first? Has anybody seen . . . ?
Precise	Do I have to read all of this? How am I going to remember all of this? Who cares about all this "stuff"?	Don't have specific answers Avoid debate Skim instead of read Take few notes	Overwhelmed when confronted with details Fearful of looking stupid Angry at not having the "one right answer"!	Don't expect me to know names and dates! Stop asking me so many questions! Does it matter? I'm not stupid!
Technical	Why should I care how this works? Somebody has to help me figure this out! Why do I have to make something— why can't I just talk or write about it?	Avoid using tools or instruments Talk about it instead of doing it Rely on the directions to lead me to the solution	Inept Fearful of breaking the object, tool, or instrument Uncomfortable with tools; very comfortable with my words and thoughts	If it is broken, throw it away! I'm an educated person; I should be able to do this! I don't care *how* it runs; I just want it to *run*!

(Continued)

Table 3.2 (Continued)

	How I think	*How I do things*	*How I feel*	*What I might say*
Confluent	Where is this headed? Where is the focus? What do you mean, imagine?	Don't take social risks Complete one task at a time Avoid improvising Seek parameters	Unsettled Chaotic No more change or surprises, please!	Let's stay focused! Where did that idea come from? Now what? This is out of control!

SOURCE: Used with permission of Let Me Learn, Inc., Center for Advancement of Learning.

itself a model of the LMLP and professional development grounded in reflective practice.

Bringing the Process to the Students

In the monthly sessions, teachers continue to build understanding of their own learning patterns and then learn how to implement the process in their classrooms. Classroom implementation begins with weeks of daily activities in which students think and share what they are doing when they learn. They also discuss the actions of familiar television and book characters, paying close attention to the tools used by the characters. For example, third and fourth graders might discuss how Abraham Lincoln and Martin Luther King Jr. used words to advance the cause of equal rights for African Americans, while Harriet Tubman used action. All three played an important role, yet each did so in a different way. High school students might discuss the characters from a TV series such as *Friends, The Apprentice,* or other "reality" shows, looking at how each character exemplifies a different approach to processing experience.

When the students are ready, they take the LCI. Additional activities help students see their patterns in action. At the monthly workshops, teachers discuss student work products and anecdotes about processes used to keep the classroom focused on understanding learning and how patterns influence ease and difficulty of certain activities. Ideas, successes, and challenges are shared, with an emphasis on constant reflection about how the teachers' learning patterns are influencing their work. In the classroom, student LCI scores may be displayed with each student's description of how he or she uses each pattern. Now familiar with the vocabulary, students can understand when the teacher says, "We are doing math problems now, so get ready to use your sequence. Those of you who avoid sequence, take a deep breath. You will need to do this activity working step-by-step." High school students meet in small groups to discuss their patterns, how they use them, and to get tips from peers about how to better access patterns typically avoided. The students are now able to view themselves and each other as equally valuable learners, creating the possibility of a real learning community in the classroom. The teacher is not only the facilitator of the community, he or she is a member, with more expertise in the content area, but an equal member in continuous learning about learning.

Case Study: The LMLP in Action in Long Island, New York

The process was introduced to a Long Island, New York, school district in 1998 with an introductory awareness session given to the entire faculty. The district's Teacher Center then decided to offer a workshop for interested teachers. Twelve teachers from all grade levels and a variety of content areas attended the six-session workshop, and a group of middle school teachers performed a full implementation with their classes. The teachers who participated in the implementation were a sixth-grade Social Studies/English teacher, who also served as one student team's homeroom teacher, and the teachers of Home and Careers. These teachers chose to implement the process because they saw it as an appropriate focus for a course of study focusing on life skills and as a vehicle for helping students achieve greater success in all classes.

The Home and Careers teachers created activities allowing students to collect data about their ways of processing tasks and to analyze tasks for needed learning patterns. For example, when the students did a cooking project, they examined where each pattern was used: sequence in following the recipe, precision in making sure all ingredients were correct and on hand, technical in executing the process, and confluence to give the finished product a "unique twist." The Homeroom/Social Studies/English teacher used student learning patterns to create groups of students with complementary patterns (one student leading with sequence, one with precision, one with technical, one with confluence). These groups completed projects together and helped each other with assignments in their other classes.

All five teachers said they experienced greater success than in previous years in achieving their goals for the students after implementing the process. They also developed greater understanding of how their own patterns both influenced the way they formulated activities and assignments and created a lens through which they viewed students. They came to understand why certain students were so "easy" (they had similar patterns to the teacher's) and others were "difficult" (their different patterns made it difficult for them to learn the ways the teacher taught). This understanding opened up dialogue allowing the teachers and students to strategize for greater learning for students and satisfaction for the teachers. The students surprised the teachers when they spontaneously told an interviewer about using their patterns in an activity that was part of a field trip to a local museum. These teachers succeeded in creating a real community of learners.

Building the Space for and With Parents

While serving as an assistant principal in the school district described above, the author discovered that the framework of the ILM was extremely valuable for understanding student disengagement and resulting disciplinary issues. After sharing insights about student difficulties with their parents, she found that parents wanted to know more about their children's ways of processing classroom experience. An introduction given at a daytime PTA meeting led to a request for a four-evening workshop, where the 12 families participating found they gained understanding of their children's difficulties in school *and* at home, and about themselves as learners as well.

Participation in the workshop required a commitment from the families to attend/participate in all four sessions, with the same parent attending all four sessions. An additional family member was welcomed if he or she chose to attend, and the child or children attended the final session. The sessions were modeled after the introductory "awareness" workshop designed for teachers. Activities were modified to make them appropriate for home use. At each session, parents participated in small-group activities focused on their own and their children's responses to various tasks, followed by a debrief of each activity. Each family received a packet containing sufficient copies of the LCI at the appropriate levels for each family member. By the end of the second session, families had LCI scores for each family member and were ready to talk to each other about their learning using the framework and vocabulary of the LMLP. In the

final session, the children and parents completed an activity sepa-
rately and then came together with each other and other families to
do a building activity in which they could reflect on their learning
patterns in action. By the close of the last session, parents and
children were ready to look at themselves, each other, and others—
including their children's teachers and administrators—through the
lens of the ILM, recognizing each as a capable, valuable, unique
learner.

A Sample Activity

The purpose of the activities, as is the case in the teacher workshops, was to provide tools for the parent to use to collect data about
themselves as learners using the framework of the ILM. A variety of
activities focused on application of the ILM, including those described
above for teachers. After two sessions, parents were ready to take the
LCI and begin to get familiar with the vocabulary of the learning
processes. Learning to view *themselves* and their learning/schooling
successes and failures through the framework was the first step to
seeing their children and others through the learning lens, opening
up possibilities for dialogue about learning within the family and
between the family and the school.

By completing the chart in Table 3.3 as a "homework" assignment, parents began applying their developing understanding of the
influence of learning patterns on the tasks of schooling that caused
household conflict.

Completing this activity allowed the parents to see how their
children's learning patterns were making it more difficult for them to
meet some requirements of school and, more important, to see how
their children needed *explicit strategies* to access patterns they tended
to avoid. Difficulty remembering to bring notes home ceased to be
evidence of a child being "irresponsible" and became evidence of
high use of the technical process. To the child, the task was irrelevant
to her interests at that moment.

Equipped with a strategy employing a "use first" pattern—for
example, using confluence to create an interesting bracelet to wear as
a reminder—the child remembered notes more often. In addition, she
also saw her difficulty as something to work on, something she could
articulate to others without shame. Mom and daughter were also then
able to explain to her teacher her need for help and space to develop
and use strategies to remember "irrelevant" tasks in the classroom.
Small-group sharing of the charts included sharing possible strategies

Table 3.3   Sample Activity for Parents

1. For the next two weeks, fill in this table, naming tasks related to school in the first column. These may include homework (short and long term, papers and projects), getting ready for school (including eating, dressing, putting on shoes, brushing teeth), remembering snack/lunch money. Do this activity with your child if you can get him/her to participate!
2. After your child takes the LCI and you have explained the four patterns (please use the Web site for help on this!), have him/her fill in the scores for each area.

********BRING THESE CHARTS WITH YOU NEXT WEEK********

School-Related Task LCI Scores:	Sequence (Planning, working step by step, order, consistency)	Precision (Details, questions, facts, research)	Technical Reasoning (Problem solving, real-world relevance, autonomous, tools)	Confluence (Unique, do it my own way, connecting to other ideas and people)

to help the children use patterns "used first" to help access patterns "avoided."

Parents who attended the workshop responded overwhelmingly that the understanding they gained about themselves and their children altered the whole family's perceptions of each other. One parent sent an e-mail saying, "It was terrific, one of the most valuable things I have learned this lifetime." The framework of the ILM gave these families a way to talk about what they were thinking, feeling, and doing to each other, and to help the students explain their ways of processing to their parents and the teachers, whose only goal was to see them learn. The parents became core members of the school learning community, able to be the partners in learning and schooling so essential for their children's success.

> ### Reflective Questions
>
> 1. How might a tool for understanding learning contribute to the growth of a learning community in your school's faculty?
>
> 2. How might shared understanding about unique ways of processing influence student peer relationships in your school?
>
> 3. How might understanding and being able to articulate your ways of thinking, feeling, and doing influence your perspective on and relationships with your students/colleagues/parents?

The ILM and Reflective Practice

The reflective practice process described in Chapter 1 includes "observation and analysis" and data collection, leading to double-loop learning. Double-loop requires a change in theories-in-use, not just a change in behavior. Teachers, students, and parents who experience the LMLP invariably report their retrospective awareness of prior theories-in-use. Comments the author has heard include the following:

- "If she can't come up with an original idea for the project, she must not be very creative."
- "The student who can't remember his times tables must have a faulty memory" (even though he never forgets his friend's phone numbers).
- "Anyone so disorganized will never amount to much."

After viewing these same children/students/colleagues through the lens of the learning patterns, these theories-in-use changed to this: "His/her patterns are different from mine, so it's difficult for me to understand why he/she has so much trouble with something so easy for me." This change opens the space for *real* dialogue about how each member of the community is processing current issues. As each member is validated in his or her way of learning and given tools to use information about learning with intention and communicating it to others, every voice can find its way into the conversation. *Real* co-construction of meaning in a relational space where all members of the community are seen as distinctive learners with essential contributions to offer can become a reality. In such a space, real solutions to the problems of educating all children are possible.

Chapter Summary

This chapter presented a framework for understanding learning, the core technology of schooling. In providing an alternative lens or mental model for observation and analysis of learning and schooling behaviors, this framework has led many school leaders to a deeper understanding of themselves and the influences on the values and beliefs guiding their practice. Leaders who understand the power of learning patterns and styles—their own and those of all members of the school community—can work with that power to create truly inclusive school/learning communities. In the next chapter, we move to the next step, focused examination and expression of the values and beliefs providing the foundation of leadership practice: the vision statement.

Notes

1. Materials and information on the Let Me Learn Process are available at www.letmelearn.org. and www.lcrinfo.com.

2. Original and continuing research on the Let Me Learn Process, including validation and reliability studies, is available at www.letmelearn.org.

Suggested Readings

Johnston, C. A. (1996). *Unlocking the will to learn.* Thousand Oaks, CA: Corwin.

Johnston, C. A. (1998). *Let me learn.* Thousand Oaks, CA: Corwin.

Johnston, C. A. (2004a). *Learning to use my potential.* Paper presented at the Pioneer Leadership Academy, University of Houston, TX, June 16–20.

Johnston, C. A. (2004b). *When you are ready to begin to make a difference.* Annual ASAH Conference, State of New Jersey, Atlantic City, November 12.

Johnston, C. A. (2005). *Power by design.* Paper presented at the EU-Sponsored Meeting of the Grundtvig Partnership, Westminster University, London, January 9–11.

Johnston, C. A., & Dainton, G. (1997). *The learning combination inventory.* Pittsgrove, NJ: Let Me Learn, Inc.

Johnston, C. A., & Dainton, G. (1997). *The learning connections inventory.* Turnersville, N.J.: Learning Connections Resources, LLC.

4

Developing a Personal Vision Statement for Building and Sustaining Leadership

Although the platform is only espoused theory, writing it usually begins a reflective process of greater depth. Writing itself has the potential to be a powerfully reflective process.

—Osterman and Kottkamp (1993, p. 880)

Reflective Questions

1. If asked, "Who are you?" how would you respond? (Answer this question before you go on to the next one.)

2. Go beyond some superficial responses, such as, "I'm a teacher, a mom, or a coach." What really defines who you are at your very essence?

3. What do you really care about most?

4. What do you passionately believe?

5. What factors, incidents, or people have influenced you the most?

6. How have they contributed to forming your beliefs and values about education and leadership? Explain in detail.

7. Why is uncovering these influences important for better understanding who you really are and what you believe?

Respond to these questions in a microlab.

Framework

Why do educational leaders behave the way they do? What determines whether or not an educational leader (e.g., principal) behaves compassionately or autocratically toward staff members? What influences one to espouse practices aimed at nurturing and supporting collegial learning communities? What influences one to translate these espoused ideas into theories-in-use? Is one's training or personality the most influential factor? What influences one to think, speak, and act a certain way about a particular educational issue? What are the major influences on educational leaders' beliefs and values about teaching and supervision? What factor(s) contribute(s) to how a superintendent, for instance, might view or perceive an educational problem? Can educational leaders change their attitudes and goals? These are fundamental questions that will not all be answered in this chapter or book. Yet a major premise of this chapter is that by uncovering and articulating beliefs and values, you can begin to understand some of the influences or precursors of your espoused theories and may even better connect them to theories-in-use. Conversely, the framework for reflection described below is aimed to stimulate thought on potential factors that might influence your espoused theories. Awareness of these influences is essential in order to articulate a well-reasoned, meaningful vision statement for leadership.

While attending a seminar in education about 25 years ago, one of the authors had the privilege of listening to B. F. Skinner, professor of psychology at Harvard and a researcher who won several awards for his contributions in the area of human behavior. During the question-and-answer period, Skinner was asked, "When people realize they are controlled, will they lose their feelings of freedom?" The renowned author of *Walden Two, Science and Human Behavior,*

Verbal Behavior, and *Beyond Freedom and Dignity* stoically responded that he didn't know (e.g., Skinner, 1976). He went on, however, to explain that his own behavior was a result of three things: his genetic endowment, his past history (his family, religious experiences, schooling, physical environment, etc.), and his present situation. He concluded by saying that he wasn't discouraged or unhappy that these factors shaped his behavior. Clearly, Skinner maintained that we are products of our environments. Although behaviorism captured the attention of the educational community for the better part of the previous century (e.g., Baum, 1994), over the last 20 or so years, cognitive psychology has offered us a refined understanding of human behavior (e.g., Seligman, 1998). The field of general semantics has also helped us, in particular, to better understand the relationship among language, thought, and human behavior (e.g., Korzybski, 1933/1995).

We have always been fascinated by some questions: "Why do we behave the way we do?" "Why are some principals (or other educational leaders) overbearing and autocratic and others collaborative and democratic?" "Why do we hold certain beliefs over others?" "What influences us to think, speak, and behave a certain way?

Figure 4.1 illustrates a model we have developed for understanding human behavior and maybe even change, although such exploration is beyond the purview of this chapter. The model, per se, is not

Figure 4.1   Model for Influences of Human Thought, Language, and Behavior

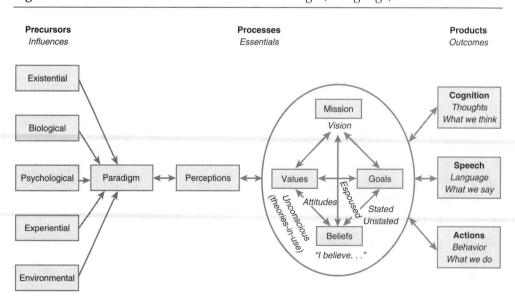

unique in the sense that we have drawn on a number of theorists and theories that are for the most part widely acknowledged. The manner, however, in which the model is framed is unique. The model consists of three sections: precursors (or influences), processes (or essentials), and products (or outcomes). The model can be best understood from left to right. Each precursor, to varying degrees, impacts on various processes that include our particular paradigm (the lens we use to view and understand our experiences), individual perceptions, attitudes, missions, and goals we set for ourselves. In turn, these processes influence what we think (our cognition or thoughts) about a given issue or situation, what we say (our language or speech), and what we do (our behavior or actions).

A fundamental assumption of the model is that the extent to which we understand the precursors or influences of our thoughts, speech, and behavior, the more likely we can function and change as needed and, equally important, understand others. We will first briefly explicate the various components of this model and then relate how the model may serve to help us develop and understand our personal vision for leadership.

As the model indicates in Figure 4.1, five influences or precursors of human thought, language, and behavior are presented. Each precursor is called a "plane" or "domain." Although space limitations preclude a complete discussion of each domain, below is a cursory overview.

Existential

Every educational leader operates, consciously or unconsciously, on an existential plane. Six existential modes for all human beings can be identified:

- Educational leaders exist "in and with the world"; that is, a deliberate and thoughtful interaction occurs between our "selves" and the world around us. In other words, we act and make decisions relative to the circumstances and situations we encounter. We react to ideas and negotiate our physical surroundings.
- Educational leaders possess a conscious self and can relate to and interact with other humans.
- Educational leaders perceive a subjective reality that is dependent on one's perspective or social situation.

- Educational leaders are transcendental in the sense that they think and experience mental, emotional, and spiritual dimensions.
- Educational leaders are temporal beings who understand that the past, present, and future form an "undifferentiated whole."
- Educational leaders possess potential for self-improvement: physically, intellectually, emotionally, and spiritually (PIES).

More concisely, educational leaders are influenced by their very nature as interactive, conscious, subjective, transcendental, temporal, physical, intellectual, emotional, and spiritual beings.

Reflective Questions

1. How does your existential self influence the lens you use to relate to others?

2. How does your existential self influence your beliefs and values?

3. Do you see any relationship between your existential self and your leadership style?

Biological

As the model indicates in Figure 4.1, the biological domain is another influence or precursor of thought, language, and behavior. Five biological modes can be described:

- Educational leaders possess specific drives (e.g., hunger, rejuvenation, procreation) and needs (e.g., food, sleep, sex).
- Educational leaders possess innate tendencies, qualities, or personalities.
- Educational leaders are influenced by their gender. In other words, we know that women and men are different biologically and that as a result they think and behave in different ways.
- Educational leaders possess unique physical characteristics that may influence thoughts and behaviors.
- Educational leaders possess talents, gifts, or natural inclinations that influence thoughts and behaviors.

More concisely, educational leaders possess drives, needs, innate qualities, physical and genetic characteristics, and natural inclinations.

Reflective Questions

1. Do genetics or biological factors influence you in any way? Explain.

2. How does this biological influence shape or influence your beliefs and values?

3. Do you see any relationship between your gender and leadership behavior?

Psychological

As the model indicates in Figure 4.1, the psychological domain is another influence or precursor of human thought, language, and behavior. This domain can be characterized by a variety of psychological theories. Clearly, a comprehensive discussion of the psychological dimension to human behavior goes beyond the purposes of this chapter. One example, however, will suffice that indicates a powerful psychological influence. William Glasser's (1999) "needs theory" finds relevance in this context. According to Glasser, all human beings have five essential needs, and all behavior is an attempt to satisfy one or more of these needs: security (physical, emotional); belonging (social approval, acceptance); freedom (choice, will); fun (enjoyment); and power (self-efficacy). A major premise is that everything a human being does is an attempt to fulfill one or more of these needs. The prime motivator is self-actualization.

Psychologically, any discussion about the nature of human thought, language, and behavior requires attention to the innate needs of human beings.

Reflective Questions

1. How does the psychological dimension influence your beliefs and values?

2. How are psychology and leadership related?

Experiential

As the model indicates in Figure 4.1, the experiential domain is another influence or precursor of human thought, language, and behavior. Two modes are identified below: the personal and the social. As Skinner indicated, one's past history and experiences are significant influences in one's life. Social experiences are powerful influences of human behavior. Interacting with others in social settings is commonplace. We see and learn about ourselves by relating with peers and others. These interactions reaffirm and/or help us to develop images of ourselves. For example, when Mary Johnson is teased by her classmates because of her dress, speech, or possibly awkward behavior, such interactions may negatively affect her self-image. Mocking or criticism both at home and school may create feelings of inadequacy and increased dependency on others for social and personal acceptance. These social experiences affect how Mary thinks about herself, how she talks about herself, and how she acts in social situations (e.g., as a social isolate). Another example is appropriate here: If you were robbed or cheated by someone of a particular ethnic group, then this experience (especially if reinforced by societal stereotypes and possibly reinforced by other people's experiences) may influence the way you think, speak, and act toward someone else from that particular group. The personal experiences we encounter (events that occur in private) also shape our perceptions of reality and ultimately our view of ourselves.

Educational leaders are influenced by their social and personal experiences.

Reflective Questions

1. How have your experiences influenced your beliefs and values?

2. How have your experiences influenced your behavior on a daily basis?

3. How have your experiences influenced your leadership style?

Environmental

As the model indicates in Figure 4.1, the environmental domain is another influence or precursor of human thought, language, and behavior. Four environmental modes can be described:

- Familial: No doubt, one's family influences behavior patterns and actions. Aside from the psychological implications of familial influence, such experiences play an enormous role in shaping beliefs and attitudes of children and adolescents. The long-lasting impact of family has also been well documented (e.g., Evans, 2004).

- Educational: Educational experiences (influences of educators and programs) are significant factors in shaping one's philosophic outlook and behavior, especially as they relate to the work experience. Early educational influences clearly have an impact on human behavior (Evans, 2004). Even educational experiences that occur later in life have a substantial influence. Someone, for instance, trained in progressive teaching methods at a teacher training institute is more likely to exhibit progressive educational practices compared with someone trained in more traditional methods.

- Religious: Although studies indicate recent decreases of religion in shaping and sustaining behavior (e.g., Neusner, 2003), religion still plays an important role in affecting many individuals (e.g., Harris, 2004).

- Societal: Societal influences are made up of six concepts:

  1. History: Historical trends, whether societal or otherwise, shape human behavior and practice (e.g., Bryson, 2003). For example, a historical event like the September 11, 2001, terrorist attack on America may have reshaped or reframed our view of the importance of making a difference in the lives of children through education.

  2. Economic: The role of economics in influencing human behavior has been documented (e.g., Sowell, 2003). For example, an economic event such as a stock market crash may affect our lives in significant ways.

  3. Cultural: Cultural influences are well researched (e.g., Sowell, 1996). For example, the type of music we enjoy may influence our beliefs and attitudes (for instance, Judy Collins's and Arlo Guthrie's music during the Vietnam War years influenced this author's antiwar sentiments and other feelings toward education and life).

  4. Political: The role of politics in shaping human behavior (e.g., Sowell, 2002). For example, a political event such as a presidential election may affect our ability to earn a living or receive a particular social benefit.

  5. Social: The dynamics of human relationships, individually or collectively (e.g., Dunn, 1995). For example, our everyday social contacts with people we work with may influence our

own beliefs and attitudes. Think of how teenagers may be influenced by their peers and by adults, too.

6. Ideas: The influence of ideology on our behavior (e.g., Weiss, 1997). For example, the idea that a group of people is considered intellectually inferior to another based upon skin pigmentation has influenced many people's thoughts and actions toward others.

Reflective Question

1. Select any two societal concepts above, and explain how they have influenced you. Provide examples.

The model described above may serve to help you develop and understand your personal vision for leadership.

Reflective Question

1. How might this model help you develop and understand your personal vision for leadership? (Share ideas with a colleague before you read on.)

Consider your responses to all the preceding reflective questions. Perhaps you realize that a plethora of factors have "shaped" (or if you prefer, in non-Skinnerian language, "influenced" or "affected") who you are, what you believe in, and what you care about or value. What are these factors, and how have they influenced you?

Reflective Activity

1. Take pen and paper to hand and record your in-depth response to the previous question. (This activity may take some time; don't rush.)

2. Pair off with a colleague, and share with each other the personal factor that has influenced you the most. Explain why. The person listening to the other will report out to the larger group describing the factor that has influenced the other person.

This model, we hope, served as a reflective instrument to examine possible factors or influences on the lens you use to perceive the world around you, which, in turn, influences your beliefs, values, and mission or vision. This vision is critical in determining how you think, speak, and act. Ultimately, such a vision will play an essential role in improving your practice and help you "gain control over" your "own behaviors in the work setting" (Osterman & Kottkamp, 1993, p. 85).

Using the preceding questions or activities as a base, answer the following reflective questions, which pertain more specifically to developing a personal vision statement for building and sustaining leadership.

Reflective Questions

1. What are your beliefs and values about learning and the learning capacity of students?

2. What are your beliefs and values about teaching and its impact on student learning?

3. What are your beliefs and values about supervision?

4. What are your beliefs and values about leadership and its role in building and sustaining learning communities?

Reflective Activity

Pair and share your responses with a colleague. Record their responses, because you'll be asked to report out to the class what you have heard about that person's beliefs and values. Let your comments be descriptive, not evaluative.

Guidelines for Writing Your First Draft of a Vision Statement

Having explored a wide array of factors or influences for one's espoused theories, we now need to articulate them precisely in the form of a position or vision statement related more specifically to leadership (we also refer to the vision statement as a "platform"). By thinking and writing about them, you will be on your way to developing and continuously refining a vision statement to guide your practice as a leader. As the opening quotation of this chapter indicates, writing a position statement is a powerful way to reflect. It is a way to purposely articulate a leadership stance that can guide one's practice as a leader. Reflection leads to more reflection as we refine our position or vision for leadership and school improvement.

We believe that your statement, especially at this beginning first-draft stage, should be necessarily broad and open-ended. Therefore we have not structured your writing with specific and detailed preset questions or guidelines. At this stage, simply follow these general guidelines:

1. Freely record your feelings, ideas, reactions, and responses to the questions previously posed in this chapter. You might want to use the activity you just completed with your colleague, described above ("Take pen and paper to hand. . . ."), as a starting point.

2. Ask yourself how these responses may relate to your role as a leader.

3. In previous chapters, you learned about your leadership and learning styles. How have your styles emerged? How can they influence your vision statement?

4. Think and reflect upon your philosophy of education, view of teaching and learning, conception of curriculum and supervision, experiences in school, and your preferred leadership style.

5. Above all else, as you write this statement ask yourself, *"How can this statement serve to support my personal learning and leadership style as I work to build and sustain a learning community?"*

MY STATEMENT

_____

_____

_____

_____

_____

_____

_____

_____

_____

_____

_____

_____

_____

_____

_____

_____

_____

_____

_____

_____

_____

_____

_____

_____

_____

_____

_____

_____

_____

_____

Reflective Questions

1. Reread what you have written. Feel free to rewrite and revise.

   Is what you have written an accurate reflection of your espoused theory for practicing leadership? How do you know for sure?

2. Try to locate two others who have similar learning and/or leadership styles and share your statement in small groups with them.

   How do they react to what you have written?

   Are your platforms similar to one another's? Explain. Revise your statement based on feedback received.

3. Locate others who have different learning and/or leadership styles to obtain their reactions.

   Do you notice any differences in responses between both groups of individuals? Revise your statement based on feedback received.

Please note that as you read others' statements, do not be critical or judgmental. Simply raise questions for discussion, as there is no one "right" response. The purpose of these sharings is to stimulate discussion, reflection, and personal refinement of vision statements. Therefore offer descriptive, not evaluative, feedback to others. Here are a few guidelines to consider as you read others' statements:

1. Have they seriously considered some of the influences described earlier in the chapter?

2. Are the statements in the platform internally consistent? For instance, if one attributes his or her current emphasis on non-traditional teaching methods to progressive teaching methods in the 1970s and 1980s, does he or she indicate similar inclinations in individual learning styles?

3. Are there apparent inconsistencies? For instance, one may advocate constructivist teaching and then rely on directive methods in one's personal classroom. Remember, don't criticize, but merely ask, "I've noticed you said _____. How does _____ relate to what you've said earlier?"

Developing a Second Draft of Your Personal Vision Statement

Keep in mind that this vision statement is a personal statement that allows you to present your views regarding education and educational administration/supervision, your philosophy, your values, your beliefs, your vision of the way schools should be, and your view about what you as a school leader would do to realize this vision. In short, the vision statement is a way for you to say what you stand for as an educational leader.

Now that you've received some feedback from others, you're ready to write a more permanent draft. Consider your learning and leadership styles, as discussed in previous chapters along with discussions of reflective practice and constructivism. Your goal is to build and sustain a sound learning community that supports good teaching and high achievement for all students. Focus on your vision of leadership that helps to accomplish this lofty goal. This vision statement will guide your practice and help you accomplish your goal.

We now offer more specific questions that should stimulate your thinking. We include questions in part based on the Educational Leadership Constituent Council (ELCC) national standards. They are commonly used to guide and accredit educational leadership programs in the United States and can also help frame your statement. Where possible,

- Support your ideas with examples and theories from the literature on leadership.
- Use examples that have inspired or influenced you.

Please remember that this activity is intended to help you articulate your own personal feelings and ideas. It is not a test of what you know, and there are no right answers. The guiding questions that follow are meant to stimulate thought. Although your statement should address the "big" ideas implied in these questions, you do not have to answer each one in sequence or at all. Allow them to guide your thoughts. Read them all and then start writing.

Guiding Questions

1. What has influenced your vision of leadership?

2. What are your goals or hopes for your students?

3. What are the types of skills, attitudes, and feelings you want students to possess?

4. What type of climate is needed to support the student outcomes you identified above?

5. What can you do to help establish that climate?

6. What are your views about teaching and learning?

7. How should instruction be organized and delivered to support the type of climate and student outcomes you desire?

8. How would you promote a positive school culture, providing an effective instructional program, applying best practices to student learning, and designing comprehensive professional growth plans for staff?

9. What is your philosophy on leadership?

10. What can leaders do to create effective schools?

11. How would you exercise leadership in your building?

12. How would you facilitate the development, articulation, implementation, and stewardship of a school vision of learning supported by the school community?

13. Provide examples of how you would act with integrity, fairly, and in an ethical manner.

14. What would the governance structure look like?

15. How would you manage the organization, operations, and resources in a way that promotes a safe, efficient, and effective learning environment?

16. What are your responsibilities as a leader?

17. What are your ideas for collaborating with all families and other community members, responding to diverse community interests and needs, and mobilizing community resources?

18. How would you seek to understand, respond to, and influence the larger political, social, economic, legal, and cultural context?

19. Offer a concluding statement.

See sample platforms at the end of the chapter that can serve as guides for your own writing. Don't feel you need to conform to the precise way these students went about writing their platforms. These statements vary in length and style as well as content. Two pages may suffice to elucidate one person's ideas, whereas another may require 10. These differences illustrate the idiosyncratic and essentially personal nature of visioning. Remain creative, and affirm your own individual style.

Class Practice

Bring three copies of the second draft of your vision statement to class. In groups of three, read each other's vision statements, one at a time. Find two people with leadership or learning styles different from yours. Provide descriptive feedback to the authors. The purpose of descriptive feedback, as differentiated from evaluative or prescriptive feedback, is to provide the reader with a deeper understanding of the ideas expressed in the vision statement (Osterman & Kottkamp, 1993).

The following strategies will help avoid the prescription/evaluation trap:

- Note logical consistencies and inconsistencies among the sections of the draft.
- Identify underlying assumptions.
- Take notes on the writer's perspective and value orientation to clarify your own positions and values.

Sample Statements

Janice Micali, a leadership candidate, offered to share the vision statement she created based on this chapter:

> There is no more prodigious challenge than that of educating children. Those of us who chose to become educators understand the awesome responsibility that comes with the task. Educators are entrusted with the greatest gift the world can offer: the future. We are sculptors; we create and mold the minds of the future world. The school, at all levels, must work together toward the common goal of educating children. It is our job to ensure that the children of this country and our school master the skills that will enable them to become functioning members of society. Educators cannot work as independent units, each of us operating with

our own agendas. Educators at every level must work together to create an environment in which children can learn how to think and express themselves.

Schools are complex places, and teaching is a difficult and challenging job. I believe that the child is the reason for the school's existence, so education must be concerned with the whole child. Learning is a continuous process that must foster academic achievement. The students should learn to set goals for themselves and enjoy a healthy self-concept. In order to achieve this, the unique abilities inherent in each child will be recognized and encouraged to ensure that the child becomes a useful, contributing member of society.

My vision will be to invite and encourage others to participate in determining and developing my vision into a shared vision that is clear, compelling, and connected to teaching and learning. With this vision, I hope to help focus attention on what is important, motivates staff and students, and increases the sense of shared responsibility for student learning and achievement. In doing so, our first step will have to be to assess the current vision in order to properly produce a "new" altered vision.

I hope that this shared vision will help create a common ground that serves to facilitate or promote action toward the realization of OUR vision. As a group, we will have to consider the challenges and benefits of the "shift." This vision will state what, how, and why we are expected to deliver it and believe in it. This vision should clearly create and sustain an environment where all students learn at the highest levels. With this vision, I hope to provide an inspiring image of the future for myself, the staff, the parents, the community, and most important, the students.

A common thread throughout this platform is that education is a process that has an end within itself: the quest for knowledge and understanding. Also, this process is one of constant reorganization, restructuring, and transformation to meet the needs of an era and the particular needs of individuals in any era. The components of a school culture that reflects my vision are instructional climate, teaching and learning, student outcomes, and leadership and governance. To understand my vision of leadership, it is necessary to define each component and demonstrate how each is integrated into the school culture, while keeping in mind that our school's goal is to aim for excellence in academic achievement, personal development, and social responsibility in a culturally diverse society.

Student Outcomes

The cornerstone of any educational vision is student outcomes. Learning is a continuous process involving many factors. It must foster academic achievement and emphasize how to learn rather than focusing only on the acquisition of facts, and the students should learn to set goals for themselves and should enjoy a healthy self-concept. To achieve this, the unique abilities inherent in each child should be recognized and encouraged. In this way, the child can become a useful, contributing member of society.

This vision is committed to developing learners who use their minds well and who are provided the requisite curriculum, instruction, assessment, support, and time. The students need to meet rigorous academic standards. The students need to learn to understand important concepts, develop essential skills, and apply what they learn to real-world problems. They should value, respect, and appreciate multiculturalism and diversity. They should become productive and moral citizens, accountable for their learning and actions. They should be prepared to meet the changing and diverse challenges of a technological society, therefore becoming technologically literate and global minded. The students should be collaborative decision makers, enthusiastic, confident, and inspired to realize their highest potential.

They should be inquisitive, curious, independent learners who can seek and obtain knowledge on their own. They should be able to work cooperatively. Students must realize the powers of persuasion but have the ability to compromise, to benefit the needs of many when working in a group. Students should go out into the world with the knowledge they learn and perform to the best of their ability. Upon leaving school, students should have a sense of direction and purpose. They should leave as independent and interdependent individuals capable of availing themselves of the opportunities to participate as ethical and productive citizens in a globally interdependent society.

My vision supports all students in realizing that they have the potential to reach high standards. I will encourage the development of self-discipline, positive self-image, strong personal values, and the respect for all school community members. I will utilize all available resources, both financial and human, to maximize the effectiveness of the school and its programs.

Instructional Climate

The realization of student outcomes is inextricably tied to the instructional climate. My vision is to truly exemplify that all students can learn. The students, staff, and parents should feel safe and nurtured. The school should be seen as a community for learning. All involved are seen as partners in the education of our children. The school will promote a climate of acceptance and mutual respect. The culture of the school will support collaboration, foster reflection, and celebrate accomplishment. Multiple opportunities for celebration of individual and schoolwide success in all areas of achievement will be developed.

It will be a school where everyone is physically and emotionally safe. It will be a safe, trusting, and collaborative environment that develops lifelong, self-directed learners. The school will provide a safe and secure environment where people enjoy learning. It will work in partnership with the community. The school will be an up-to-date technological and physical environment conducive to learning. To ensure a safe environment, a code of appropriate behavior will be developed, agreed on, and modeled by all. Consequences for inappropriate behavior will be clear and consistently enforced by all members of the school community.

The students' work will be displayed throughout the building and classrooms. Classrooms will be print- and material-rich environments that encourage the different learning styles of all children. For the classroom to be an effective learning environment, the teacher and student must possess joy for learning. The "arts" will also be incorporated into the school, so that the students can pursue their creative sides with music and art. The school will also offer an extensive afterschool program that will include sports, tutoring, enrichment, homework help, mommy/daddy and me classes, and the arts.

The school will also be supported by professional development and workshops. This will allow the staff to have the opportunity to grow, self-assess, reflect, and collaborate. My vision is to support teachers by providing new-teacher training, mentor teachers, team teaching, classroom intervisitation, and weekly peer observations in which classrooms will serve as demonstration sites for specific organizational and instructional practices. This will provide a forum for the exchange of ideas, concerns, problems, positive and negative experiences, teaching styles, and creativity, and support interaction amongst the staff. In addition to this, there will also be an open-door policy that will create a direct link between the staff, school community, and me. Ample professional resources will be housed in the professional library, so as to support all aspects of the professional development program.

My vision will also provide ample opportunity for parents to become involved. There should be active parental involvement in decision making and in learning policies. There will be a parent room in the building for parents to receive literature about current issues. It is here that they will be able to speak with the parent coordinator, find/locate extensive resources in multiple languages, and read the schedule for upcoming parent workshops and even translators. The parents will be encouraged to get involved with the school as often as possible. They will be viewed as full and equal partners in the educational process and in the daily life of the school.

Teaching and Learning

The instructional climate is the framework that supports the teaching and learning in the building. Students will have a variety of learning experiences in and outside of the classroom that will develop their ability to become lifelong learners. This curriculum will reflect multiple instructional strategies that will accommodate different needs and learning styles. Students will be grouped heterogeneously according to grade level. I'd like to try to keep class size at a maximum of 20 students for Grades K through 2, and 25 for Grades 3 through 5.

Each child will be encouraged to progress at his or her own developmental level and speed. Each child's curiosity and creativity will be nurtured. To achieve an environment conducive to learning, the teacher must expect appropriate behavior fostering respect and consideration for oneself and others.

The assessment model will incorporate a spectrum of tools so as to support a holistic approach to evaluation. Teachers will be required to keep portfolios on each student. They will accumulate many observational notes, running records, student exhibits, and assessments in these portfolios. Every aspect of the instructional program will focus on the diverse needs of the students; on their academic, social, and personal growth; and on high standards for student achievement. The school community will be committed to maintaining the same high level of expectations for all students, while acknowledging the individual differences among students meeting the standards, and to encouraging and nurturing student enthusiasm for learning.

Opportunities for enrichment, intervention, and extracurricular activities will be offered throughout and after the school day. After-school activities provide a perfect bridge between the students, parents, and staff to the school and its community. Another way to promote this bridge will be to hold events like talent shows, music concerts (chorus, band, and dance), and sports competitions, which will get parents into the school to watch their children perform and/or compete.

An excellent offspring of the afterschool recreational activities will be a schoolwide volunteer service program that will encourage students to give back to the community (which may, in turn, create more community support). I will propose a per-session job for a teacher who will be responsible for placing and periodically supervising students in a variety of facilities and organizations. This will give students the opportunity to build self-esteem and self-worth while offering a helping hand in the community.

Leadership and Governance

Essential to the realization of my educational vision is a model of leadership that supports collaboration and includes and encourages multiple perspectives. My leadership style will be seen as proactive, flexible, and reflective. I will model values, beliefs, and behaviors. Two specific values that will be encouraged and modeled are honesty and integrity. In this model, the principal will be responsible for providing the time and the structure for students, staff, parents, and other school community members to openly participate in some aspects of the governance process.

I will be committed to a collaborative approach of leadership and sustain a focus on the fundamental belief that student achievement must drive all aspects of the educational process. I will actively work to secure the resources needed to support the instructional process and to develop and sustain a supportive and open relationship with the community. I will share in both the joys of our successes and in the struggles of our setbacks.

Leaders should be able to listen to, affirm, and give value to the thoughts and actions of staff members. Therefore I will offer support and insight by being visible in classrooms and throughout the building. I will work to maintain an atmosphere of cooperation by allowing for my staff to meet and exchange ideas and concerns. Criticism will be constructive, and all in the school community will have input in the decision-making process.

The school leader will have the responsibility to see that teacher observations in the classroom setting will be geared toward personal growth and will not focus on evaluation. Teachers will be expected to meet with leadership in planning conferences and postconferences, where they will choose and react to their own plans for growth through the process.

Leadership will also have the primary responsibility for maintaining a clean and orderly environment within the school building, while emphasizing the need for the entire school community to take ownership in that task.

The schools of the future must be equipped to handle complex problems. I think it is no longer possible for one person, in the form of a principal, to manage all these problems on his or her own. It is essential for the principal to create school management teams that help develop new ideas and add twists and turns to existing ideas in order to improve the school. I think that the key to success is the team concept composed of individuals who truly dedicate themselves to their profession and to children.

A staff that works together with the parents can only help the development of the school. It is important for the staff to expend energy working together on a shared vision, rather than against each other. My staff and I will try to achieve all of this by raising expectations and academic rigor for all students, increasing student engagement through better instruction and added support services.

This vision statement hopes to connect to the powerful dreams and positive values of staff, students, and parents.

Patricia Andersen, another leadership candidate, shares her personal vision as follows:

Leadership in the schools of today is a particularly complex issue. We live in a constantly changing, highly technological age, one in which the abilities to use critical thinking skills and to obtain and evaluate newly discovered, up-to-the-minute information are of paramount importance. The skills and strategies required for even the most basic tasks are considerably more complicated than those required in past decades. It is my belief that we, as a society, owe our children the best education we can provide, one that suits the needs of every child and prepares each one to face the challenges of the future. Not only do schools need to promote each student's cognitive development, we must also consider the development of the child as a unique individual, focusing on the child's psycho-social, emotional, and moral dimensions as well. Teachers and administrators must work closely together to encourage youngsters to open doors to new opportunities and experiences, to foster the development of skills enabling students to become lifelong learners, and to inspire creativity and courage to explore innovative ideas. Embarking upon a career in educational leadership requires both a strong sense of purpose and a clear vision if we are to initiate necessary reforms and help create the magnificent schools our students so richly deserve.

All children are learners by nature. They may learn at different rates and through a variety of modalities, but they will learn nonetheless. I am confident that all children are capable, competent students who will achieve success, given proper support and experiences that will enable them to discover new concepts and construct meaning. Students will not only reach the high standards as set by New York state, they will come to establish goals of their own choosing in consultation with their parents and teachers, thereby becoming active participants in the decision-making process that is a part of authentic learning behaviors. This will breed confidence in their abilities as learners, a strong work ethic, and the knowledge that learning is within their control.

Students will develop keen language skills, concentrating not only on proficiency with the four traditional strands of literacy development—speaking, listening, reading, and writing—but also on the expanded strand of computer literacy and research skills. Mathematical thinking, spatial concepts, and problem solving will likewise be areas of attention, as will the content area subjects. Furthermore, there will be an emphasis placed on physical education and the arts, with numerous opportunities to explore talents in those areas. Students will be guided to an understanding of the connectedness of these subject areas and how they are related to their own lives and experiences. Special attention will be devoted to the development of higher-level thinking skills, such as making inferences, evaluating information, and making judgments.

A spirit of discovery, wonder, and enthusiasm for seeking new insights will be encouraged throughout the school. Students will come to realize the important contributions each person provides to the learning community as a whole. In addition to the independence they will gain as learners, they will simultaneously develop the necessary skills to work cooperatively with others. It is my hope that each child will develop a positive self-image, strong principles, a sense of self, and respect for diversity and the value of community. I want students to enter the wider world empowered to meet the challenges that lie ahead with creativity and confidence, eager to take their place in society as productive citizens.

To enable students to reach the goals outlined above, the atmosphere of the school will be of vital importance. It is my intention to cultivate a feeling of teamwork in the school community, including students, parents, teachers, administrators, and staff, as well as volunteers from the community outside of the school. All will be welcome participants in the processes of learning and shared decision making, working together toward a common goal. Their contributions will be viewed as unique and valuable, generating mutual respect and trust. Active, patient listening and honest communication will be necessary qualities. Tolerance and appreciation of diversity will naturally be supported in such an atmosphere. As principal, I will model and encourage such behaviors by providing opportunities for the school community to practice them on a regular basis.

The role of the family in education must not be overlooked. Parents will be invited to serve on a variety of teams to engage in a dialogue discussing the needs, policies, and goals of our school, such as the School Leadership Team, PTA, and smaller, subject-specific committees, to ensure that their voices and suggestions are heard. Flexibility in arranging conferences between teachers and parents throughout the year will be upheld, for these connections are critical to success. Moreover, parent workshops/programs will be presented at night and on weekends to further increase parent involvement and assist them in their efforts to have a meaningful impact upon their children's education. Such programs will include, but not be limited to, strategies to support "at-risk" students, language barriers, needs of diverse learners, discussions of policy and curriculum changes, and the like. Links to social services and private agencies will be made possible as well. Moreover, planning special events such as sports outings and school picnics will help increase our sense of community.

Similarly, teachers will have a significant influence on school policy and decision making as well. Their insight, experience, and professionalism will be honored. Again, I will institute teams to investigate options related to instructional practices, educational resources, new methods of assessment, and the like. I will encourage teachers to poll students in order to further inform such decisions. As principal, I intend to be a visible presence, making myself available to all members of the school community for discussing concerns, progress, and new ideas. Upon advocating the same approach for teachers and their relationships with students and parents, I believe we will witness supplemental growth of our community framework.

Community outreach is still another critical component of expanding this climate of school community and teamwork. As the saying goes, "It takes a village to raise a child." I will seek out affiliations with local community organizations and businesses not only as a resource to bring into the school but also as a means of providing service to the greater community outside our doors. Of course, volunteers from the community who would like to support our efforts toward learning inside the school building will be welcome additions. This may come in the form of donations, guest speakers, or tutors. However, I will endeavor to bring the school outside into the community at large. Perhaps teams of students, teachers, and parents could work on beautifying a community garden or provide tutoring at a neighboring school. Such interaction could only serve to enrich the students' educational experiences, support character development, and improve community relationships.

I envision the school building as an appealing, print-rich environment, captivating visitors and everyday community members alike. Hallways and classrooms will serve as showcases of student discovery, progress, and accomplishment. Special honors and awards will also be displayed. Special talents will be celebrated at annual art shows, talent shows, concerts, and dramatic/dance performances. The school building will be a vibrant place that is full of energy.

In my opinion, teaching and learning are two sides of the same coin. One cannot exist without the other, for they are interactive processes. To develop the necessary skills of a lifelong learner, students must be exposed to a broad assortment of experiences that promote discovery, dialogue, and reflection. Teachers guide their students in their attempts to activate prior knowledge and to make connections with other topics and experiences. Utilizing various strategies and resources, teachers construct student-centered activities that enhance active student engagement. In so doing, the teacher as facilitator accommodates the diverse needs of students and allows them to capitalize on different learning styles and ways of expressing learning. Conscious, thoughtful planning on the part of the teacher is crucial to success. Assessment will be based upon a wide array of tools and measures, enabling teachers to consider various factors when evaluating student progress. Among them are standardized tests, teacher-generated tests, written assignments, group projects, class activities, informal observations, portfolios, presentations, and journals.

To support teachers in their efforts to provide their students with the highest-quality learning experiences possible, reflective practice and ongoing professional development will be endorsed. Time will be devoted to these practices on a regular basis. Teachers will be thoroughly involved with selecting topics of interest for professional development and in the planning of such workshops to ensure the needs of the staff are sufficiently being met. Professional development activities will be hands-on in nature, inviting active participation. Intervisitation schedules will be planned to give colleagues the opportunity to observe one another's methods and engage in a meaningful dialogue about them. Add to that my commitment to pursue opportunities for intervisitation between other schools in the region as well, to further open the dialogue regarding innovative teaching practices. Correspondingly, it will be incumbent upon me as a school leader to stay abreast of advances in the field of education to better serve the school community and to model the drive to never stop learning for my staff.

The school will be organized into a cluster configuration, enabling a more personalized "school within a school" experience for the intermediate school student. Classes will be heterogeneously selected. The children in the cluster will share the same major subject teachers, who will meet twice per week for the purposes of planning interdisciplinary units, holding parent conferences, and discussing trends, teaching strategies, and student observations/class dynamics. Enrichment and intervention classes will be worked into the school day, and extra opportunities will be provided for these services through afterschool programs as well.

In my capacity as a school leader, I will endeavor to be a proactive, principle-centered individual. The school's driving impetus will be to maintain high expectations for all children. Collaboration with the members of the school community will enable the development of a teamwork approach to building and sustaining a learning community. I will rely upon the counsel and support of the entire team—administrators, teachers, staff, parents, and students—to share the responsibility for making decisions, implementing policy, and managing day-to-day school operations. Providing ample opportunities to meet and discuss our progress and ever-changing needs is a necessary factor for a successful partnership. Open communication must be valued by all and fostered at all levels. All voices must be cherished.

Leading by example is of profound significance if one is to gain the trust and respect of those one presumes to lead. In that spirit, I have developed a brief list of the principles I wish to act upon in my efforts to exercise leadership in an ethical manner. I am confident that with a philosophy of leadership such as this, we will enjoy the fruits of a supportive and successful school community:

- Seek input from all members of the team.
- Communicate with others honestly and openly.
- Practice active, patient listening to promote the true exchange of ideas.
- Treat team members with respect.
- Foster the development of healthy relationships among team members.
- Be fair to all parties when making decisions.
- Admit your mistakes without delay, and begin to correct them just as quickly.
- Be willing to experiment with new ideas; encourage others to do the same.
- Never stop learning.
- Pursue personal excellence, and support others in their pursuits.
- Nurture the potential for growth.
- Be visible for, involved with, and accessible to the team.
- Strive for balance.
- Practice and encourage creativity and critical thinking.
- Reflect on the ever-changing needs of the team on a regular basis.
- Maintain a sense of humor and a positive attitude.

Chapter Summary

In this chapter, we presented a framework for reflection aimed at stimulating thought on potential factors that might influence your espoused theories. We then offered a guide to the development of your personal vision statement based on your espoused theories and a process for obtaining descriptive feedback from your colleagues. Keep in mind that your vision statement is a work in progress.

Suggested Readings

Green, R. L. (2005). *Practicing the art of leadership: A problem-based approach to implementing the ISLLC standards* (2nd ed.). Columbus, OH: Pearson Merrill Prentice Hall.

Osterman, K. E., & Kottkamp, R. B. (1993). *Reflective practice for educators: Improving schooling through professional development.* Thousand Oaks, CA: Corwin.

Schussler, D. L. (2003). Schools as learning communities: Unpacking the concept. *Journal of School Leadership, 13,* 498–528.

Sergiovanni, T. J. (1994b). Organizations or communities? Changing the metaphor changes the theory. *Educational Administration Quarterly, 30,* 214–226.

Westheimer, J. (1999). Communities and consequences: An inquiry into ideology and practice in teachers' professional work. *Educational Administration Quarterly, 35,* 71–105.

PART II

Building a Learning Community and a Community of Learners

Strategies and Techniques

In the first section of this book, we focused on the "personal." We provided the reader with a background on the major concepts, *reflective practice* and *constructivism*, underlying the strategies and techniques that we believe will assist in building an enduring community of learners and a community of practice at all levels of the school. Then, we explored the importance of understanding who you are and what you believe and how to model, share, and explore this knowledge and its acquisition with the other members of your learning community. Chapter 2 looked at personal leadership styles and how to determine your strengths and weaknesses, personality preferences, motivations, and the impact you have on others. Your personal learning styles and how to explore those of the rest of the school community was the theme of Chapter 3. In Chapter 4, we offered a guide to the development of your personal vision statement based on understanding the influences on your life, how you and others lead and learn, and your espoused theories. Finally, we presented a process for drafting your personal vision and for obtaining descriptive feedback from your colleagues.

The second section of the book is an outgrowth of the first—the two are inseparable. It is your enhanced personal knowledge of who you are as a leader and learner, the awareness of how others lead and learn, and your espoused theories that will facilitate transforming them into theories-in-use. This transformation takes place through the learning and use of strategies and techniques that facilitate the development of a community of learning and practice. Chapter 5 focuses on developing interpersonal skills, primarily communication and listening skills. Chapter 6 introduces a series of opening exercises and techniques to assist groups in getting group work off the ground. In Chapter 7, we offer an array of problem-solving strategies and techniques that promote constructivist learning and leading for all school constituencies. Last of all, a case study that represents a composite of our experiences demonstrates how an actual community of learners and a community of practice can be developed.

5

Bridging the
Personal and the
Interpersonal

*Far too often, we equate communication with the ability to frame
ideas and information in an interesting or persuasive manner.
With the primary focus on the speaker, too little attention is paid
to the listener.*

—Osterman and Kottkamp (2004, p. 80)

*One of the ironies of modern civilization is that, though mechan-
ical means of communication have been developed beyond the
wildest flight of the imagination, people often find it difficult to
communicate face-to-face.*

—Bolton (1979, p. 4)

The goal of this chapter is to begin to enable you to take your
enhanced personal knowledge and your espoused theories and
develop them into theories-in-use. Sharpening the interpersonal skills
that are based on listening and communication skills is the first step
that will facilitate that growth. You already experienced a sample of

the kind of feedback that enhances communication in the process of writing your personal vision statement. The descriptive feedback that you shared with your colleagues is representative of responses that we believe foster communication. The second step is to develop the ability to make your wishes and needs known without putting the listener on the defensive. These strategies are called "assertion messages."

We believe that it is important to practice these interpersonal skills first in the safe environment of a classroom or workshop. The second step is to try them out at work or at home, followed up with a discussion of successes and challenges with classroom or workshop colleagues. At this point, the habits and strategies will begin to be internalized.

As many of you have probably learned along life's road, we cannot control the other person's or group's response. As we previously discussed, we cannot *make* change happen. We can only learn and use strategies that encourage open interchange and subsequent problem solving.

Listening Skills

Introduction to Listening and Listening to Introductions

One of the authors often begins the first leadership class with the simplest of listening exercises. She asks each candidate to turn to his or her neighbor. Each person has 1 minute to respond to a series of simple questions about his or her professional life. Each person talks for a minute. No one can take notes, and no questions or discussions are allowed. At the end of 2 minutes, each candidate recounts to the whole group what he or she has learned about the colleague. As the students try to recount the information the colleague shared, they are amazed to see how little they remember and how inaccurate some of their recollections are. This exercise awakens the class to the need to develop listening skills.

This activity is also the first opportunity to introduce practices that we think can begin to be applied across the school spectrum. School leaders can be introduced to each other in this manner at the district level; a new school leadership team can begin their first meeting this way. Administrators can share this exercise with their staff when personnel changes take place; and then the teachers can adapt it for their students. Children of any age can enhance their capacity to learn if they improve their listening skills. The suggestions below are

Table 5.1   Building a Community of Practice

Adult Practice	
• College classroom	• Candidates describe where and what they teach and their past teaching experience, their reasons for taking the course, and their professional aspirations.
• Leaders with other leaders	• Leaders talk about their leadership positions and schools, their goals, aspirations, and challenges.
• Professional development	• Participants explain, if appropriate, where and what they teach, the reason for choosing the workshop, and what they hope to learn and take back to their schools or classes.
• Group or team meeting	• Staff explain why they are participating, what roles they would like to play, and what goals they see for the group.
• Parent meeting	• Parents or guardians describe who their children are, share something positive about their personal or children's experience in the school, and bring up a concern they would like addressed.
Student Practice	
• K–12 classroom	• Students give their names, tell what class they were in and teacher(s) they had the previous year, and what their favorite and most challenging subjects are. The students mention one thing they would like to learn this year.

included to give you an idea of the types of questions that can be used at each level to increase participants' awareness of their listening skills (see Table 5.1).

Communication Techniques

Awareness of how carefully we listen is the first step in improving our listening skills. The next step is to acquire techniques that will facilitate effective listening. Half of the battle is your ability to focus on the speaker; the other half is to communicate to the speaker that you are listening carefully and to verify that you have understood what the speaker is trying to express or convey.

The three types of techniques that follow promote effective listening and understanding (see Table 5.2).[1] Listening techniques, the first

Table 5.2   Communication Techniques

Listening	Nonverbal Clues	Reflecting and Clarifying
"Uh-huh" "OK" "I'm following you" "For instance" "And?" "Mmm" "I understand" "This is great information for me" "Really?" "Then?" "So?" "Tell me more" "Go on" "I see" "Right"	Affirmative nods and smiles Open body language (e.g., arms open) Appropriate distance from speaker—not too close or too far Eye contact Nondistracting environment Face speaker and lean forward Barrier-free space (e.g., desk not used as blocker)	"You're angry because . . ." "You feel . . . because . . ." "You seem quite upset." "So, you would like . . ." "I understand that you see the problem as . . ." "I'm not sure, but I think you mean . . ." "I think you're saying . . ."

category, have a dual purpose: They encourage the speaker to continue, and indicate that you are following carefully; they support your listening by inserting brief comments that relate to the content of the message. Nonverbal clues, the second category, have similar effects: They clearly indicate to the speaker the listener's attention and free both the speaker and listener from physical distractions and barriers that hinder interactions. The third category, reflecting and clarifying techniques, is the most important in terms of verifying understanding, and the most frequently omitted. Most miscommunication results from the speaker saying one thing and the listener hearing another. How often do children say, "You aren't listening to me!"? Adults are often not as open and hear from their own perspectives without verifying. So many misunderstandings can be avoided through the use of these techniques.

Barriers to Communication

Another category comprises a set of reactions that have deleterious consequences for both the listener and the speaker: They discourage people from expressing themselves openly; they interrupt and often end the narration; they put the speaker on the defensive; and they prevent the listener from hearing the speaker's perspective. These barriers to communication are referred to as "spoilers" and "high-risk responses" and as a general rule should be avoided (see Table 5.3).[1]

After reading the list, students often wonder whether there is anything they *can* say. We offer two suggestions to this reaction. The speaker is most often looking for a sounding board, not advice. Therefore the less said, the better. By the time he or she has finished the story, the speaker has usually at least begun to work out his or her feelings or response. The organization of the speaker's thoughts frequently leads to resolution without assistance. The use of the listening and communication techniques is the most effective reaction. Nevertheless, some of these barrier responses can be effective in particular circumstances—for example, questioning can help clarify what is being expressed. Our recommendation is to use them sparingly and carefully.

Most of these barriers to communication are part of our theories-in-use and are ingrained in our language and habits. Ongoing practice is therefore vital to change. This practice can begin with the following exercise, which is appropriate for all levels of speakers and listeners,

- in leadership classes,
- between leaders and staff at meetings,
- for parents or guardians to prepare for listening to their children, and
- for children to practice with each other.

Adult and Student Class Practice

Everyone should find a partner and face that person. Each person will take a turn listening and responding to his or her partner. The goal is to use the communication techniques to foster an effective interchange and to avoid falling into any of the barrier traps. Keep Tables 5.2 and 5.3 handy to facilitate the learning process.

Table 5.3   Barriers to Communication

Barrier Type	Examples

1. Judging
  • Criticizing
 	
  • Name calling and labeling
 	
  • Diagnosing—analyzing motives instead of listening
 	
  • Praising evaluatively
	1. Judging
	  • "You are lazy; your lesson plan is poor."
	  • "You are inexperienced/an intellectual."
	  • "You're taking out your anger on her;" "I know what you need."
	  • "You're terrific!"

2. Solutions
  • Ordering
 	
  • Threatening
 	
  • Moralizing or preaching
 	
  • Inappropriate questioning or prying
  • Advising
 	
  • Lecturing
	2. Solutions
	  • "You must . . ." "You have to . . ." "You will . . ."
	  • "If you don't . . ." "You had better or else."
	  • "It is your duty/responsibility; you should . . ."
	  • "Why?" "What?" "How?" "When?"
	  • "What I would do is . . ." "It would be best for you."
	  • "Here is why you are wrong . . ." "Do you realize . . ."

3. Avoiding the other's concerns
  • Diverting
 	
  • Reassuring
 	
  • Withdrawing
 	
  • Sarcasm
	3. Avoiding the other's concerns
	  • "Speaking of . . ." "Apropos . . ." "You know what happened to . . ."
	  • "It's not so bad . . ." "You're lucky . . ." "You'll feel better."
	  • "I'm very busy . . ." "I can't talk right now . . ." "I'll get back to you."
	  • "I really feel sorry for you."

Step 1: Each partner should take a minute to think of a current personal or school dilemma.

Step 2: Partner No. 1 will recount his or her dilemma.

Step 3: Partner No. 2 will show interest in the speaker's situation by using the listening and nonverbal techniques and avoiding the barriers (Tables 5.2 and 5.3).

Step 4: Partner No. 2 will choose reflecting and clarifying techniques to verify what he or she heard and to show understanding of the feelings expressed.

Step 5: Partner No. 1 will give feedback on how well Partner No. 2 used the techniques.

Change partners, and repeat the cycle. Each cycle should take no more than 5 minutes.

Personal Practice

During the next week, target someone who is going to share an experience, problem, or dilemma with you. It can be a spouse, a child, a colleague, or a student. Keep copies of Tables 5.2 and 5.3 on hand, and practice your listening and communication techniques. When the interchange is completed, reflect on what worked well and what areas need improvement. Jot down notes so that you can exchange your reflections on the experience with your colleagues or classmates. You can first share by e-mail, on a discussion board, or in a chat room, and then in class. You may feel a little uncomfortable at first using these techniques. Remember that because the listeners are involved in their virtually uninterrupted sharing, they won't be aware of your novice status as active listeners.

Assertion Messages

Our focus in this chapter has been primarily on listening skills and the techniques that will encourage others to communicate. However, it is equally important to be able to express one's feelings and thoughts in a manner that transmits needs without putting the listener on the defensive. This type of communication is called an assertion message. You have already used one strategy in the vision-writing process that is integral to assertion messages: descriptive feedback. A description of content or behaviors allows the listener to hear a nonjudgmental perspective. In addition, many of the readers of this book are already familiar with the conflict resolution techniques that are used with students. One of the principal tenets of the conflict resolution process is the use of the "I" message instead of the accusatory "you" as each party explains his or her version of the events in question. Description from the "I" point of view is also a central principle of assertion messages.

Robert Bolton, in *People Skills* (1979), provided a comprehensive description of how to develop effective three-part assertion messages. He posited that assertion messages are the thinking being's response when one's space is violated, as contrasted with the "fight" or "flight" of our prehuman ancestors. We include verbal responses as well as actions in the behaviors that invade the asserter's personal space. Bolton referred to the goal of assertion messages as getting the other to change the behavior that is intruding on the asserter's territory. At the same time, he said that the message defends one's own turf without violating the other's space. The goal is for the recipient to devise a solution that maintains his or her own self-respect while meeting the asserter's needs. We believe that if we focus on the possibility of joint problem solving to produce a solution, it no longer is a win-lose situation, but a win-win one. Bolton also cautioned not to use assertion messages in high-risk situations. His advice was that the method should meet the following criteria:

1. There is a high probability that the other will alter the troublesome behavior.

2. There is a low probability that you will violate the other person's space.

3. There is little likelihood of diminishing the other person's self-esteem.

4. There is low risk of damaging the relationship.

5. There is a low risk of diminishing motivation.

6. There is little likelihood that defensiveness will escalate to destructive levels.

Reflective Questions

1. Try to think of a situation where you felt someone intruded on your space and you did not assert yourself. What happened?

2. Think of a circumstance where you asserted yourself when you felt your space was violated. What happened?

3. What conclusions do you draw from your experiences?

The basic assertion message is comprised of three parts:

1. A nonjudgmental description of the behavior that is violating the asserter's space

2. An explanation of the asserter's feelings

3. A clarification of the concrete and tangible effect(s) of the other person's behavior on the asserter

The following examples will give you an idea of professional and personal situations where assertion can be effective:

- You are the parent of a teenager who has been coming in late with his friends on weekends. They make a lot of noise, wake you up, and then you cannot fall back to sleep. You feel like getting up right then and saying, "How can you and your delinquent buddies be so inconsiderate? Any more noise and you're grounded for the rest of the weekend!" This response would combine three barriers in two sentences: judging (delinquent buddies), moralizing (inconsiderate), and threatening (grounding). Instead, you decide, after the most recent incident, to wait until the next evening after you both have had some rest, and you say,

  1. Description: "When you come home late at night with your friends and make noise"

  2. Feelings: "I get quite annoyed"

  3. Effects: "Because it wakes me up, I can't fall back to sleep, and then I'm tired the whole next day"

- You share your classroom with another teacher, who uses it during your prep and lunch. When you return, the blackboard is always full of writing. You do not have enough time before the class begins to erase it well and put up your next class's information. You feel like saying, "It is every teacher's responsibility to clean up the classroom before the next teacher comes in. Please make sure that you erase the blackboard before I return from lunch and prep." This response contains moralizing (teacher's responsibility) and ordering (make sure that you erase). Therefore you decide to try the following message:

1. Description: "When I get back from prep or lunch and the board has writing on it"

2. Feelings: "I feel frustrated"

3. Effects: "Because the class gets antsy while I erase it and try to get my information up"

- You are a person who likes all your ducks in order. Even in conversation, you like to finish your complete thought before discussing it with anyone. Your colleague is spontaneous and less structured. She always interjects her ideas before you get a chance to finish. It drives you crazy! You feel like saying, "Can't you control yourself? It's really rude to interrupt someone in the middle of a sentence." You know that that response is judgmental (can't you control yourself?) and moralizing (it's really rude). So you decide to say,

1. Description: "When you interrupt me in the middle of a sentence or thought"

2. Feelings: "I feel irritated"

3. Effects: "Because I lose track of my ideas and forget what I was saying"

A few final hints when using three-part assertion messages:

- Make sure your description of the behavior is specific.
- Be descriptive and objective—don't draw inferences or be judgmental.
- Be as brief as possible—concentrate on one behavior.
- Make sure that your assertion is not "displaced"—that you are not using a small issue instead of facing a bigger one, or ignoring small issues until they create a major issue.
- Don't take out your frustration with one person on another— yelling at your wife when you're angry with your boss. (Bolton, 1979)

Adult and Student Practice

This exercise is valid for all members of the school community, from staff to parents and guardians to children:

Step 1: Break up the class into pairs.

Step 2: Each person writes a three-part assertion message that he or she would like to communicate to someone.

Step 3: Partner No. 1 will describe the context, explaining who the message receiver is. Partner No. 1 will then share his or her message. Partner No. 2 will take the role of the receiver.

Step 4: Partner No. 2 will provide descriptive feedback on the effectiveness of each message.

Step 5: Repeat the process with Partner No. 2 sharing his or her message. Partner No. 1 will be the receiver.

Step 6: Each pair will report out something they learned from this practice about creating assertion messages.

Personal Practice

This exercise is valid for all members of the school community: During the next week, target someone who has a behavior that you feel invades your personal space. It can be a spouse, a child, a colleague, or a student. Try to prepare and write down the assertion message beforehand. After you have used the assertion message, reflect on how it worked. How did the other person respond? What choices did you make that were effective? What would you do differently if you had the opportunity to repeat the assertion? Jot down notes so that you can exchange your reflections on the experience with your colleagues or classmates. You can first share by e-mail, on a discussion board, or in a chat room, and then in class. You may feel a little uncomfortable at first using these messages. Remember, again, that because the other person is immersed in what you are saying, he or she won't be aware that you are using a formula.

Chapter Summary

This chapter was the first step in making use of the self-knowledge acquired in the first section. The listening and communication skills in this chapter are all prerequisites for effective group work. Groups cannot communicate or solve problems if they do not listen to each other, if they put up communication barriers, and if they do not assert their perspectives effectively. We are now prepared to learn the skills that get group work off the ground.

Note

1. These tables and exercises have been adapted from Sullivan, S. & Glanz, J. (2005). *Supervision That Improves Teaching: Strategies and Techniques* (2nd ed.). Thousand Oaks, CA: Corwin.

Suggested Readings

Suggested readings for Chapters 5 through 7 are included at the end of Chapter 7. Many of the readings contain ideas that are relevant to more than one of these chapters.

6

Getting Started

Setting the Tone

Vitality springs from experiencing conflict and tension in systems which also incorporate anxiety-containing supportive relationships. Collaborative cultures are innovative not just because they provide support, but also because they recognize the value of dissonance inside and outside the organization.

—Fullan (1999, p. 27)

In Chapter 5, we introduced and gave you the opportunity to practice some techniques that address communication between individuals and that also have an impact on our communication in groups. One of the assumptions in Chapter 5 was that the ability to listen to and hear different perspectives and to voice one's own is the first building block of communication. An assumption of this chapter is that communicating in groups is facilitated by processes that promote understanding and expression of differences. Thus in this chapter, we go to that next level: the group. If we want to build a school learning community and a community of learners, the ability of the different constituents to work fruitfully in groups is essential.

Before we can address differences, however, the tone has to be set. The group has to "break the ice" and "get off on the right track." In our years of facilitating faculty and staff groups, we have accumulated a "bag of tricks" that have been effective in a variety of settings. Many of them can be adapted easily to children and parents. "Getting off on the right track" strategies help set the tone, as do "icebreakers." Although some overlap exists, "icebreakers" focus more on building relationships, and "getting off on the right track" techniques center on processes that facilitate the functioning of the group. You were already introduced to a few strategies in the listening exercises you practiced in Chapter 5.

This chapter is divided into two sections: In the first section, we present samples of icebreakers. They precede ideas to provide a structure for the group, which makes up the second part of this chapter. The goal of all of these suggestions is to stimulate your thinking. How can you adapt them for your context? How can you use them with children? With parents? What ideas do they give you for your own original icebreakers? We recommend that the instructor in a college class model as many of these exercises as possible at the beginning of several classes.

Note that icebreakers may not be fashionable in this era of accountability. Nonetheless, 5 or 10 minutes at the beginning of a workshop, retreat, or a group initiating a collaboration can set a tone that actually saves time in the long run.

Reflective Questions

1. What activities have you been involved in where icebreakers have been used? What was effective in their use? What was of little value? Why?

2. What meetings or workshops have you attended where the use of icebreakers might have improved the sessions? Explain.

Getting to Know You: Icebreakers

These suggestions are for groups where most of the participants have not met before or are superficial acquaintances.

Introductions to Listening

In addition to serving as an introductory listening skills exercise, the "introductions" format that we introduced in Chapter 5 is a simple and effective way for a group to become acquainted.

Find Someone Who . . .

Figure 6.1 provides an example of this simple, enjoyable, and effective icebreaker, which can be used with a variety of groups. In Figure 6.2, we have added some suggestions that illustrate how this exercise can be easily adapted for an academic year opening workshop or meeting. Variations of this icebreaker can also be used with a small class of students on the first day of class.

Directions

You will have 10 minutes to complete this exercise. Find a different person for each qualification. Note next to the attribute the name of the person and why he or she qualifies for this statement. When we regroup after 10 minutes, you will share something interesting you learned about one of the participants.

Personal Practice

Think of a meeting or a group with which you will be interacting in the near future. Create your own "Find someone who . . ." or adapt the example to fit your group. Remember that you can use it in a K–12 classroom. The rules and timing have to be very clear for children. A stopwatch after 1 minute and/or a group circle to limit movement might be helpful. It could even be used as a diversity exercise for children to learn about family and cultural customs of their classmates. Take notes on what worked and what needs improvement, and share with your class.

Figure 6.1   Find a Person Who . . .

1. is the oldest in his or her family.

_____

2. has a pet.

_____

3. plays a musical instrument.

_____

4. has seen the last movie that you watched.

_____

5. has more than five brothers and sisters.

_____

6. can speak two languages.

_____

7. has a new baby in his or her home.

_____

8. has a birthday is in the same month as yours.

_____

9. was not born in this country.

_____

10. was born in the same birth order in his or her family as you were (e.g., first-born, middle child).

_____

Figure 6.2   Find a Person Who . . .

---

1. traveled out of the state of _____ this past summer.

   _____

2. traveled out of the country this past summer.

   _____

3. has found a way or ways to feel more peaceful, relaxed, and less stressed.

   _____

4. has done something to help you out that you appreciate.

   _____

5. helped resolve a conflict recently.

   _____

6. knows a teaching technique for getting students to pay attention or listen when they are distracted or are distracting others.

   _____

7. has a hobby or interest that you didn't know about.

   _____

8. learned something this past summer that can improve classroom instruction and/or improved his or her leadership skills.

   _____

9. ate a new food or cooked a new dish this past summer.

   _____

Which One Isn't True?

This icebreaker can be used with a group that is slightly or some-what acquainted. It will not work well with a group that is meeting for the first time. Each person has a card on which he or she writes three or four statements about himself or herself, something interesting or unusual if possible. One of them is not true, while the other two or three are. Figure 6.3 is an example.

Figure 6.3   Which One Isn't True?

1. I was born in Guadalajara, Mexico.

2. I was a championship swimmer.

3. I play two musical instruments.

4. I have three children, two of whom are twins.

Directions

Distribute 3 × 5 cards to all participants. No names should be written on the cards. Ask the participants to write three or four (the facilitator decides how many) interesting, unusual, or significant statements about themselves. One of the statements will be a lie. The facilitator collects the cards, shuffles them, and reads one card. The participants try to figure out who wrote the card. Since this exercise is somewhat time-consuming, the facilitator can read a small number of the cards and continue after a break or at another meeting.

Personal Practice

In the next few weeks, try to practice this exercise. Try it out at a meeting, in a class, or at a social gathering. Take notes on what worked and what needs improvement, and share with your class.

Complete the Thought

This icebreaker is the simplest and the most creative. You can take any thought that stimulates reflection and open a meeting or a class in this manner. The possibilities are endless. Another approach is to write a word on a blackboard or a chart and ask the group to say what this word brings to mind. We first observed this icebreaker at a meeting at Central Park East Secondary School in New York City. The goal of the meeting was to do a "Descriptive Review" (Himley, 2000) of a child and her work. Thinking about a word really set a reflective tone for the subsequent discussion. A few examples of phrases and sentences are the following:

- If I were a flower, I would be _____ (because)
- If I were an animal, I would be _____ (because)
- My happiest school memory is . . .
- My most frustrating school memory is . . .
- The word *fulfillment*
- The word *conflict*

Directions

Bring in the first half of a sentence that might relate to the topic of a meeting or the class. Write or say the phrase, and ask the group to go around in round-robin to complete the sentence. If a participant is not ready, he or she can pass. The same process applies to a word. These icebreakers are also very effective with children. The sentence completions do not even have to be changed. The words can apply to any subject area or any class discussion. The word *rules* could begin a discussion of class rules. If a classmate is ill, the day could be started with a word related to the students' feelings and concerns.

Different icebreakers abound in the nonprofit and staff development literature. We have provided a few samples. We have avoided most of those that some define as "touchy-feely" and have included examples that we believe are fun and informative and are applicable or adaptable to the entire learning community. You can also create your own or do a "Google" search on the Internet under "icebreakers."

If you feel pressed for time, you can begin a meeting asking each person to share a positive and negative feeling about the topic at hand, or something each person would like to achieve in the collaboration. What is important is setting a tone of openness.

Site Practice: All Adults, Children

Think of original examples of phrases, for example, "If I were . . ." and appropriate words to use in a variety of professional contexts: as a leader in a group, with colleagues, at a parent meeting, or with students. Practice a phrase or word in at least one context, and share the reactions and results with your class.

Getting Off on the Right Track

Now that we have "broken the ice," we can proceed to learn strategies that will foster the building of a collaborative, productive environment. In this section, we offer exercises that get the group process off the ground. Note that we do not explain the different roles in a group or on a team nor do we delve into the organizational structures and roles assigned in group development. The strategies we present set the tone within whatever structure exists or is being created.

Ground Rules

All groups that meet on an ongoing basis need a set of understandings about how to interact with each other. We believe that if the group itself creates the set of norms, the participants will respect and adhere to them. This belief about a group's buy-in to its own creations is valid from kindergarten through adulthood. Therefore the directions for ground rules and the sample that follows can be adapted for all ages and all ongoing groups. If time is of the essence, you can distribute a sheet that lists sample ground rules (see Figure 6.4). The group can then use these ideas as a springboard for their own. We avoid this approach unless time constraints are paramount because it reduces reflection, creativity, and ownership. Some groups may need to brainstorm a large number of ideas and then narrow them down. The rules should be revisited with some frequency and modified as needed. They should be posted in the meeting room, and group members should have their own copies. One of their most important functions is to avoid blaming and finger-pointing. They permit reference to a rule rather than to a person.

Figure 6.4   Ground Rules

1. _____

2. _____

3. _____

4. _____

5. _____

6. _____

7. _____

8. _____

Suggested Rules:

1. One person speaks at a time.

2. Stay on task/focused.

3. Be concise and to the point.

4. Keep an open mind; appreciate differences.

5. Avoid side conversations.

6. Provide constructive feedback and receive it willingly.

7. Keep confidences, and assume others will.

Brainstorming

Although ground rules set the tone for "brainstorming," which is an initial search for solutions to a question or problem, precise parameters for this particular technique are needed to ensure "unexpurgated" participation. And since brainstorming is a process that is essential to ongoing group work, we offer a set of brainstorming guidelines that can be adapted to any school context, from kindergarten to a meeting with a local senior citizen group (see Figure 6.5).[1]

Figure 6.5   Brainstorming Guidelines

1. All ideas are valid and should be listed.

2. It is quantity, not quality, that counts.

3. The "further" out the ideas, the better.

4. No criticism or judgment of ideas at this stage.

5. No clarification or seeking of clarification.

6. Build on each other's ideas.

7. Do not categorize or attribute ideas to groups or individuals.

8. BE CREATIVE AND HAVE FUN.

Stages of Group Development

Groups and teams often become discouraged when resistance, conflict, and other barriers arise. In our socialization, many of us learn that conflict is "bad" and a sign of failure. In fact, conflict can be a sign of healthy growth and, if handled effectively, may engender more development. Michael Fullan (1999) believes that groups composed of people of differing views learn more from each other and can be more creative and productive than like-minded groups. We agree—provided the participants truly listen to each other. People tend to "underlisten" to those with whom they disagree and "overlisten" to those who agree with them.

When a group begins meeting, it is crucial that the participants be aware that teams pass through different stages of development. Arbuckle and Murray (1989) developed a model illustrating four stages of team development (see Figure 6.6). We think that the most important feature of this model is the legitimization of questioning and, above all, of conflict in at least three of the four stages. We recommend that the facilitator of the group or team discuss these stages as a part of "getting off on the right track." The knowledge of the inevitability of doubts and conflict can help set a tone of openness and honest questioning that can be crucial on the road to group performance.

Figure 6.6   Stages of Team Development

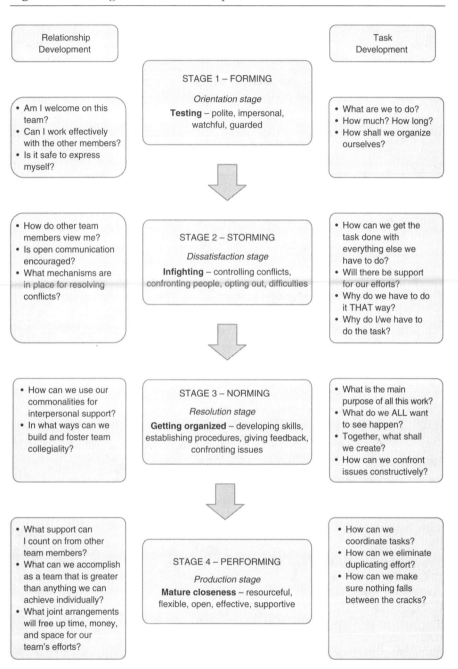

NOTE: Arbuckle and Murray (1989) describe the questions that arise in each stage of development with respect to relationships and tasks in the group.

SOURCE: Adapted from *Building Systems for Professional Growth: An Action Guide*, 1989, by Margaret A. Arbuckle and Lynn B. Murray. Reprinted with permission from WestEd.

North, South, East, and West:
Understanding Preferences in Group Work

In Chapters 2 and 3, we learned about our personal leadership and learning styles. The following exercise in Figure 6.7 presents a variation on the approaches already presented. Why are we

Figure 6.7   Choosing Your "Direction"

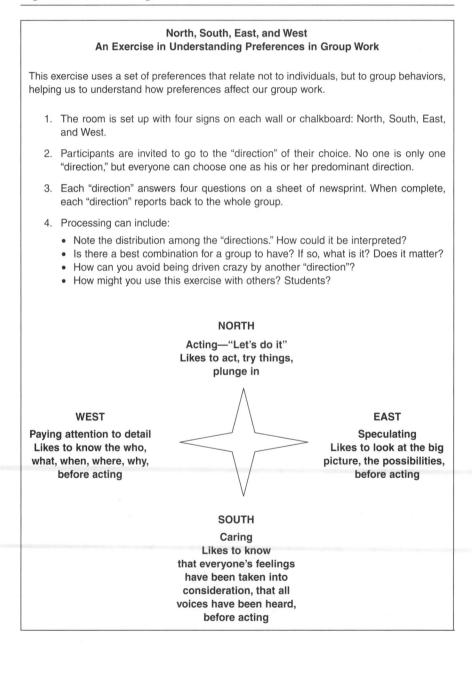

North, South, East, and West
An Exercise in Understanding Preferences in Group Work

This exercise uses a set of preferences that relate not to individuals, but to group behaviors, helping us to understand how preferences affect our group work.

1. The room is set up with four signs on each wall or chalkboard: North, South, East, and West.

2. Participants are invited to go to the "direction" of their choice. No one is only one "direction," but everyone can choose one as his or her predominant direction.

3. Each "direction" answers four questions on a sheet of newsprint. When complete, each "direction" reports back to the whole group.

4. Processing can include:
    - Note the distribution among the "directions." How could it be interpreted?
    - Is there a best combination for a group to have? If so, what is it? Does it matter?
    - How can you avoid being driven crazy by another "direction"?
    - How might you use this exercise with others? Students?

NORTH

Acting—"Let's do it"
Likes to act, try things,
plunge in

WEST

Paying attention to detail
Likes to know the who,
what, when, where, why,
before acting

EAST

Speculating
Likes to look at the big
picture, the possibilities,
before acting

SOUTH

Caring
Likes to know
that everyone's feelings
have been taken into
consideration, that all
voices have been heard,
before acting

presenting yet another perspective? First, this exercise is done in groups for groups. Although each individual chooses preferences, he or she immediately physically identifies with a group in order to process the choices and questions as part of a group. Second, this exercise is not time-consuming. It can be used to facilitate group work for an individual session of staff development. Participants can easily "turnkey" the process after using it just once. Since it is based on the Myers-Briggs Personality Inventory (Meyers & McCaulley, 1985), we include a simplified adaptation of the inventory to compare your choice of directions with those of the brief questionnaire. This exercise works with all adult groups and with older students. How could you adapt it for younger children?

As with the leadership and learning styles protocols, everyone is encouraged to apply the personal and group knowledge to problem-solving efforts. Any group assignments involving two or more people should consider group behaviors in forming committees. Group participation should also reflect the different preferences.

Analyzing Your Style

After every participant has chosen a "direction," each person responds individually to the four questions in Figure 6.8 on the same sheet of paper. Each "direction" group then lists the individual

Figure 6.8   Analysis of My Style

---

1. **What are the strengths of my style? (four adjectives)**

2. **What are the limitations of my style? (four adjectives)**

3. **With which style do I find it most difficult to work? Why?**

4. **Tell the other "directions" what they need to know about us so that we can work together effectively.**

---

responses. The group then agrees on the major findings for each question. Each "direction" shares out its composite responses.

My Problem-Solving Styles

This questionnaire (see Figure 6.9) is based on the Myers-Briggs Personality Inventory. The four categories of the questions and responses correspond with the North, South, East, and West preferences (see Figure 6.10).

After everyone has determined the scores for each problem-solving style, the facilitator can chart the group's preferences to determine the consistency between the "directions" the group chose and those that emerged from the questionnaire. Awareness of the preference configuration of the group, including their strengths and weaknesses, helps in deciding group roles and creating a balance in the composition of committees.

Adult Site Practice

In the next week or two, complete "North, South, East, and West" and the preference survey with a group with which you work. Discuss with the group how the exercise informed their understanding of their interactions. Ask them what they might do in the future with this new knowledge. Take notes on the whole process, and share your reflections with the class.

Coming to Consensus

One of the most misunderstood decision-making techniques is reaching consensus. Many people think that consensus means that everyone is in complete agreement. They also think that if a group decides to use consensus as their method of choice for decision making, no other approach can be used.

- Reaching consensus does NOT mean that everyone is in complete agreement or agrees to the same extent. It means that all participants concur that they can live with the decision.
- The agreement also signifies that everyone can support the decision because no important needs or values are compromised.

Figure 6.9 What Is Your Problem-Solving Style?

An Informal Preference Survey

Instructions: Below are five sets of words or phrases. Trusting the first thing that comes to mind, rank the items in each set from 1 through 4 (1 = most preferred, 4 = least preferred). In each set, be sure to write a different number next to each item. There are no "right and wrong" or "better and worse" answers.

1. Things I consider in solving a problem:

   a. _____ Views of those involved

   b. _____ Views of experts

   c. _____ Relevant data

   d. _____ Personal experience

2. How I usually approach a problem:

   a. _____ Explore historical background

   b. _____ Collect evidence

   c. _____ Try a solution

   d. _____ Talk to people

3. The way I like to interact with others:

   a. _____ Interview

   b. _____ Challenge

   c. _____ Convince

   d. _____ Inform

4. I like problem solving best when I:

   a. _____ Take decisive action

   b. _____ Weigh alternatives

   c. _____ Gather complete data

   d. _____ Explore the causes

5. The statement that best expresses my view of problem solving:

   a. _____ "To be successful, a solution must be acceptable to everyone involved."

   b. _____ "We have a lot to learn from our past experiences."

   c. _____ "Solving most problems comes down to figuring out cause-and-effect relationships."

   d. _____ "In the real world, you often have to solve a problem without a complete understanding of its cause."

Scoring Instructions: Each item in each of the five sets corresponds to one of four problem-solving styles. To score the survey, write your numerical rankings in the appropriate spaces below. Then total the numbers in each column. It may be easier to write the answers across the columns (1a, 1b, 1c, 1d).

1a _____	1b _____	1c _____	1d _____
2d _____	2a _____	2b _____	2c _____
3c _____	3d _____	3a _____	3b _____
4b _____	4c _____	4d _____	4a _____
5a _____	5b _____	5c _____	5d _____
Total _____ (D)	Total _____ (P)	Total _____ (De)	Total _____ (C)

Figure 6.10   Four Problem-Solving Styles

Instructions: The labels *Diplomat, Professor, Detective,* and *Champion* describe four typical problem-solving styles. **Your lowest score on the survey indicates your preferred style.** The second lowest score indicates your "backup" style. Each of us has some of the traits of each style, although one style usually predominates. This survey is designed to help you recognize the strengths and avoid the pitfalls of your preferred style.

Diplomat (D)

- Interested in reaching consensus
- Learns best from talking to those involved
- Often values opinions more than facts
- Focuses on practical solutions
- Can be very persuasive
- Needs to guard against "groupthink" and shortsightedness

Professor (P)

- Interested in underlying concepts and theories
- Seeks lots of historical background information
- Learns from relationships to other situations
- Values detachment from the issues
- Relates to others by giving and getting information
- Needs to guard against indecision and impracticality

Detective (De)

- Interested in finding the cause of the problem
- Focuses on relevant facts
- Prefers to make direct observations of situations
- Tends to follow a consistent method or process
- Tries to establish clear cause-and-effect relationships
- Needs to guard against inflexibility and insensitivity to people

Champion (C)

- Interested in results
- Finds a solution by trying one out
- Wants to achieve success without help from others
- Trusts his or her instincts
- Good in crisis situations, when there is no time for analysis
- Needs to guard against impulsiveness and uncooperativeness

- Consensus can be reached only when all concerns are on the table.
- Consensus decision making is not appropriate in all situations or contexts.

Before learning how to reach consensus, it is essential to understand the different decision-making methods, their advantages and disadvantages, and how to decide which method to use and when to use each (see Figure 6.11).

Figure 6.11   Four Major Decision-Making Methods

Method	Advantages	Disadvantages
1. Minority (can consist of one person)	Quickest	Low creativity Low commitment Can take a long time to implement
2. Majority	Quick Commitment of more than half	Creativity can be limited Limited commitment Polarizes people Can take a long time to implement
3. Consensus	High creativity High commitment Short time to implement	Takes time, patience, and communication
4. Unanimous	High creativity High commitment Short time to implement	Rarely occurs Takes time, patience, and communication

Class Practice

To clarify which type of decision method works in a school context, individually fill out the brief questionnaire in Figure 6.12. At times, two methods may have justification. Discuss the choices made and the reasoning behind them.

Figure 6.12   Recommending a Decision-Making Method

Directions: Check the box(es) that indicate(s) the decision method(s) you recommend.

Situation	Decision Method			
	Minority	*Majority*	*Consensus*	*Unanimous*
1. A subcommittee needs to make a recommendation to the principal.	☐	☐	☐	☐
2. The principal is looking over a recommendation from a committee he or she appointed.	☐	☐	☐	☐
3. A nation elects a new president.	☐	☐	☐	☐
4. A bomb threat is reported to the principal.	☐	☐	☐	☐
5. A four-person subcommittee chooses a committee facilitator.	☐	☐	☐	☐
6. After all leadership team members have given input to the school budget, the district tells the principal to make a final 5% reduction on the total by the following day.	☐	☐	☐	☐
7. A leadership team establishes ground rules for the committee.	☐	☐	☐	☐

Now that we have clarified the different decision-making methods and their appropriate use, we maintain that wherever possible, reaching consensus should be the method of choice. The initial time investment pays off in the results: long-term commitment, brief implementation time, creative solutions, and a satisfied staff.

In the next chapter, we will be presenting an array of problemsolving techniques and strategies. However, we first describe here an overarching process for reaching consensus within which several problem-solving and decision-making techniques can be employed. Conversely, this process can be included as part of a districtwide planning model. The primary goal of this model is to gain consensual commitment to a decision.

Facilitator's Role

1. *Describe the problem to be solved or the decision to be made.* Think in terms of needs, not solutions. For example, your teenage son and daughter have both asked to use the only available car for the evening. They are arguing over who needs it the most and who has the right to it. Their destinations are in opposite directions. The problem or need isn't the car, but a means of transportation to get to their destinations. You learn that your son has a date and your daughter is going with a group of friends, one of whom lives next door and has her own car. The teenagers were defining the problem in terms of a *solution*: the family car as the means of transportation rather than the need to get to their destinations.

2. *Explain why consensus is needed for the decision.* Verify that this decision is appropriate for reaching consensus. Does time exist, or can it be made to build consensus?

3. *Determine guidelines for the decision.* Brainstorm the essentials and desirables for the guidelines. The following analogies clarify this process.

   - You are in the market for a new car. What are the essentials (what you cannot do without) and desirables?
   - Your school leadership team is having a retreat. You need a site for the retreat. What are the essentials and desirables?

4. *Evaluate the options in light of requirements.* At this point, a decision-making process from Chapter 7 can be determined.

5. *Facilitate the consensus-reaching process.*

6. *Confirm team or group members' commitment to the decision.*

7. *Plan action steps, follow-up, and assessment.* Most schools and districts have planning outlines that include the "what, how, when, and where" of planning.

Class Practice

Divide into groups of four or five, with each group preferably combining learning or problem-solving preferences. Each group will decide on a school-based problem or need to be resolved. The members will go through Steps 1 to 3. During the week, after reading Chapter 7, each participant will determine which problem-solving method(s) he or she thinks is/are appropriate for the group. During the next class, the groups will reconvene, decide on a problem-solving strategy, and complete Steps 4 through 7. Depending on technological facilities, each group will present orally and on paper the results of their process (a Smart Board would be ideal for the presentation).

Site Practice: All Adults, Adaptable for All Children

Choose a decision-making group with which you are involved. Ask permission to guide the group through the decision-making process or adapt the process to make a classroom decision with students. Begin with a decision on whether or not to use consensus. Take notes on what worked in the process and how you would handle it differently with the same or another group. Share the results and your analysis with the class.

"Thinking Out of the Box"

We conclude with this exercise because it bridges icebreakers, getting off on the right track, and problem solving (the focus of Chapter 7):

- It can serve as an icebreaker for new groups.
- It can serve as a team-building exercise.
- It can stimulate thinking for visioning and problem solving.

The primary goal is to free participants to "think out of the box," to inspire unorthodox, creative ideas. We have used it as an opening exercise for personal and group visioning. Many of our students bring it back to their school classrooms to motivate children (who often solve the problems more quickly than adults because they do not feel the same mental constraints).

Directions

The goal of this exercise is to encourage you to think of original, creative ways of solving problems. We have prepared five stations, each containing a problem to be solved. The obvious answer is probably not a valid one. You may also discover a solution different from the one we envisage. The main clue is to "think out of the box," that is, to find solutions that are unusual and imaginative. You will have 1 minute at each station. When time is called, you must go to the next station. Do not reveal your answer to any other group; that means do not touch the materials—discuss and imagine the solutions. Also, each group will choose a reflector who will observe and jot down notes on how the group interacts and will report out his or her observations at the end of the exercise. We will begin with a sample problem to be solved as a whole group.

Connect all the dots below using four connected, straight lines:

```
  •   •   •

  •   •   •

  •   •   •
```

Solution: Thinking out of the box is realizing that the lines can literally go "outside of the box."

Station One

Set up: Line up six clear glasses. Fill the three on the left with colored water. All glasses should be right next to each other, with no gap between glasses.

Task: By moving only one glass, arrange glasses so they alternate, one glass with water, one glass empty.

Solution: Lift second glass of water, pour liquid into middle glass of the empty three, and replace glass. Out-of-the-box-thinking is that you can lift one glass and pour.

Station Two

Set up: Present a long board or a pole.

Task: If it takes exactly 16 minutes to cut the board into four pieces, how long would it take to cut the board into five pieces?

Solution: It takes three cuts to make four pieces, and four cuts to make five. Thus each cut takes 5 minutes and 20 seconds. Five pieces would take four cuts, or 21 minutes and 20 seconds. Out-of-the-box-thinking is to not be confined to thinking that you divide four pieces into 16 minutes.

Station Three

Set up: Write these numbers on the blackboard: 8 5 9 1 6 3 0

Task: In what order are these numbers arranged?

Solution: The numbers are arranged alphabetically. Out of the box thinking is to think beyond numerical order.

Station Four

Set up: Line up five coins horizontally and six coins vertically in the shape of a cross.

Task: By moving only one coin, create two rows with five coins in each row.

Solution: Take one coin from the row of six, and stack it on the point of intersection. Thinking out of the box is to realize that a coin can be lifted.

Station Five

Set up: Present a round cake and a large knife.

Task: Using only three cuts with the knife, how can you cut the cake into eight equal pieces?

Solution: Use two vertical crossing slices to create four pieces. Then, use one horizontal slice to make eight slices. An alternative is to cut the cake into four pieces, and then stack them for the final cut. Thinking out of the box is to think beyond cutting the cake on the top.

Site Practice: All Adults, Adaptable for All Children

Try this exercise out in a classroom or in a group with which you are working if the group is initiating a project where brainstorming for creative ideas is in order. For the classroom, you can do a "Google" search on the Internet for "brainteasers" to find all kinds of substitutions for stations we provided. Take notes on what worked in the process and how you would handle it differently with the same or another group. Share the results and your analysis with the class.

Chapter Summary

In this chapter, you were introduced to a series of strategies designed to get a collaborative decision-making process off the ground in almost any school environment. Most of the models presented apply to all faculty and staff groups, parents, and often to children, with or without adaptation. What still remains to be discussed is how groups can get to "yes"—that is, what strategies and techniques promote reaching consensus and solving problems? Chapter 7 addresses that question.

Note

1. These guidelines are similar to those in *People Skills* (Bolton, 1979) and *Communicating in Small Groups* (Beebe & Masterson, 2000). Consult these texts for an expanded explanation.

Suggested Readings

Please refer to the Suggested Readings at the end of Chapter 7.

7

Getting There

The concept of constructivist leadership is based on the same ideas that underlie constructivist learning: Adults, as well as children, learn through the processes of meaning and knowledge construction, inquiry, participation, and reflection.

—Lambert et al. (2003, p. 35)

You should never worry about your good ideas being stolen in educational reform, because even when people are sincerely motivated to learn from you, they have a devil of a time doing it. Transferability of ideas is a complex problem of the highest order.

—Fullan (1999, p. 63)

What do problem-solving techniques and strategies have to do with the transferability of ideas in educational reform? We agree with Michael Fullan (1999) that detailed written descriptions, videos, and site visits cannot capture the essence of reform. It is the conditions, processes, and interactions that spawn and nurture reform that cannot be explained or replicated—thus the need for every school and team to learn a host of problem-solving strategies and techniques to allow them to create their own conditions, processes, and interactions to foster change and growth. This belief in the necessity that "every tub must sit on its own bottom" (Hurston, 1996) is consistent with Lambert et al.'s (2003) concept of constructivist leading and learning where reciprocal processes, equity and spirituality, and reflection form the leading and learning community.

In this chapter, we present problem-solving strategies that promote constructivist learning and leading. These particular strategies and techniques have proven effective in our and others' work in schools. Again, most of these techniques are appropriate or adaptable for interactions with all school staff, parents, and children. We have culled some of them from corporate environments, some from progressive school protocols, and others from urban school district repertoires. Whereas the current high-stakes testing environment limits the time for reflective problem solving in schools, we have often streamlined the strategies. We feel that the time required for the more complete versions might discourage some staff from trying them out.

The first section of this chapter provides a set of general techniques that we have found useful in almost any situation where a decision has to be made or a problem solved. The simplicity of the versions presented is a major reason for their versatility. They are all useful with adults and children of all ages. The second smaller group of tools is often used in corporate environments. We offer versions that we have found appropriate to school environments given time and resource constraints. The following tools are presented in this chapter:

A. All-Purpose Techniques
   1. Nominal Group Process
   2. Brainstorming Alternatives and Techniques
      a. Chalk Talk
      b. Post-its
   3. The Fishbowl
   4. Microlab
   5. Descriptive Review
   6. Small-Group Consultancies

B. Corporate Techniques
   1. Pieces of the Pie
   2. Rating and Ranking
   3. Force Field Analysis
   4. The Fishbone
   5. Double Reversal

All-Purpose Techniques

Nominal Group Process

Countless times, we have found ourselves pulling this technique from our repertoire to narrow down options quickly and consensually. The title derives from the principle that the group is "nominal" (in name only). Since members are supposed to brainstorm individually and write down their own ideas first, it begins as an individual assignment (Beebe & Masterson, 2000). We will first outline the full process and then demonstrate how a simplified version applies to multiple situations.

Nominal Group Process

Purpose:

To gather and rank various solutions to a problem.

Time Frame:

Approximately 30 to 40 minutes.

Procedure:

1. Begin with a clear written statement of the problem to be addressed (express the need without hidden solutions).

2. Ask each person to spend about 5 minutes writing ideas and responses on cards or a worksheet.

3. Form groups of four to six and have everyone report out round-robin within the small groups, each person contributing one idea. A member from each group writes each new idea on a chart or chalkboard. Continue taking turns until all ideas are posted. Ideas may be clarified as you go or clarified when all ideas are charted. Clarification is aimed at making the ideas understandable, not changing or eliminating them.

4. Ask participants in the groups to list on cards the best four, five, or six ideas (whatever number seems to produce a suitable range). List these ideas on a separate chart.

5. These ideas may be further ranked by having individuals give each of them a rating of 1 to 5, with the ratings totaled for each item.

We have modified two stages of this process to meet the needs of different situations. In the first modification, the individual brainstorming and subsequent charting can take place in a whole group with the round-robin posting of suggestions. We have found that the most effective way to rank a large group of ideas is to have each participant rank his or her top three or four choices. The group can check off or place small geometrical stickers on the chart or chalkboard. The facilitator circles the ideas with the highest number of votes. The group then decides whether everyone can "live with" the winning ideas. When time is of the essence, ideas can be brainstormed as a whole group and then ranked. For example, one of the modified versions of the nominal group technique can be used to come up with ground rules.

One of the greatest advantages of this process, in any of its forms, is that everyone's ideas are validated, included, and therefore heard. The result is usually that individuals are more likely to accept the group preferences because of this democratic process.

Vignette

One of the authors was working with the leadership team of a somewhat dysfunctional institute within a large middle school. This particular institute was composed of a group of very diverse individuals with different perspectives and ideas (as most groups are). First, we refocused the theme of the institute. The next task was to set up goals for the year to implement the theme effectively. Little time remained in the meeting. The author volunteered to facilitate a brainstorming process using the Nominal Group Process. Each member contributed one possible goal in round-robin. We continued until all ideas were exhausted—about 15. Each participant then chose five ideas. The five that received the most votes became the goals. The process was quick, and everyone left satisfied that his or her ideas had been considered.

Brainstorming Alternatives and Techniques

The following techniques are either alternatives to the brainstorming technique presented in Chapter 6 or can be used to supplement basic brainstorming.

Chalk Talk[1]

- *Instructions to group:* I am going to write a statement or question on the board. As soon as I am finished, you may begin coming up to the board to write a response to my statement. You may respond as many times as you like, and you do not have to write a response at all. You may also write a response to something written by another group member. We will have chalk talk for ___ minutes (choose the time allotment based on the number of participants, somewhere between 5 minutes for a group of 5 to 10, to a maximum of 15 minutes). The only ground rule is that there is no talking during Chalk Talk.

- *Facilitator:* Write an open-ended statement or question on the board that focuses on an issue currently concerning the group. A few examples are: What would it look like if we had full equity in our school district? Our fourth graders are not achieving the results we want on the reading test because _____. How can we maintain the arts in our schedule given current literacy and math requirements?

- *Debriefing:* First, the process: What was it like for you? Did anything surprise, impress, bore you? How might you use this process in your work? Second, the content: What did we find out about our ideas on this issue? What similarities can we build on? What differences can we resolve? Where can we agree to disagree?

Post-its

Many of the techniques you have been learning can benefit from the use of Post-its. For instance, in the "Chalk Talk" exercise, the ideas and comments can be written on chart paper and taped to the wall. Pads of Post-its can be placed near the charts. Subsequently, people can post additional ideas, clarifications, and comments that can be discussed at a future meeting. It is often beneficial to chart the problem-solving strategies and leave them on the walls in meeting rooms or on hallway bulletin boards. If a pack of Post-its is readily available, the conversation can continue.

Example

One of the authors has used Chalk Talk in retreats and workshops where time is not quite as restricted and participants have more time to reflect on a topic.

The Fishbowl

The Fishbowl can serve a dual role: either as a follow-up or as an introductory activity. It can be used either to discuss ideas generated in small groups in a large-group setting or to provide feedback to a small group that is modeling a role play, simulation, or another group process. The Fishbowl is particularly adaptable to the K–12 classroom.

Example

When we teach supervision of instruction to leadership candidates, we use a very precise role play form to practice supervision skills.

Students read about the process and observe a video before trying it out. Nonetheless, we have found that the most effective preparation is when a set of volunteers actually perform the role play in a Fishbowl. The rest of the group see the process in action before attempting it themselves and provide feedback to the volunteers.

The Fishbowl

Purpose:

1. To be a follow-up to small-group discussions. To provide a forum for reporting out, sharing, and discussing the ideas generated in small groups.

2. To model a new process. Volunteers model to learn the process and receive feedback. The goal for the observers is to learn from the models' experience.

Time Frame:

The Discussion Fishbowl should be given a precise time limit; 10 or 15 minutes should be sufficient. The Model Fishbowl also should not take more than 10 or 15 minutes and should be abbreviated when necessary. Additional observations from the outer circle in the Model Fishbowl exercise should be limited by going in order and allowing only one comment per person.

Procedures:

Discussion Fishbowl: Place one chair per small group in a circle in the middle of the room. Provide an additional chair. Each small group chooses a representative for the circle to report on the group's discussion. The rest of the group observes without participating in the debriefing. If a group observer feels strongly about making a particular point, that person can sit temporarily in the additional chair in the circle to express that point. The observer then returns to his or her seat to free the empty chair.

Model Fishbowl: Volunteers model a particular role play, simulation, or process. The players sit in the middle of the room surrounded by the rest of the group. The model can be videotaped. Once the modeling is completed, anyone in the outside group can make observations. If a number of observers want to comment, it is preferable to go around the outside circle in order, allowing the group members to pass if they wish.

Microlab

Microlab[2] is a term for a planned and timed small-group exercise that addresses a specific sequence of questions and promotes active listening skills in the process. Its structure helps equalize communication and withhold judgment. It affirms people's ideas and helps build community.

Example

We use the microlab in all our leadership classes, in facilitating retreats, and in workshops. When we begin leadership or supervision classes, we want candidates to share the experiences they have had with leaders and supervisors. By asking a series of questions in which each person speaks without interruption about his or her experiences, the groundwork is laid: The participants get to know each other in a meaningful way, and the group and instructor become aware of the spectrum of experiences. Candidates talk about positive and negative experiences and their feelings and opinions about those experiences, and they begin talking about what they would do differently.

Site Practice: All Adults, Adaptable for Most Children

Over the next few weeks, practice two of the first three techniques at your school. If you work in the classroom, adapt one technique for children and use another with an adult group. Otherwise, practice two techniques with adults. Take notes. How did they work in the contexts in which you used them? Which were most appropriate for adults? Which adapted well for children? What changes would you suggest for future interactions?

Descriptive Review

In the early 1990s, one of the authors heard about a unique process that Central Park East Elementary School in New York City was using to look at individual students and their work. A large number of alternative schools had adapted the process "Descriptive Review of the Child" from Patricia Carini's Prospect Center for Education and Research in Bennington, Vermont, during which a facilitator guides a teacher's description of a child. Questions and comments from participants enable the teacher to see the child from new and different perspectives (Cushman, 1996). The full process is extraordinarily valuable for work with adults as well as with children. It is also time-consuming. We have simplified the protocol to broaden its use and usefulness in the current high-stress environment. A brief vignette about its versatility will follow our abbreviated version.

Microlab

Purpose:

The aim is to help participants, through a timed small-group exercise, learn more about themselves and others, deepen the quality of collegial sharing, and get input on specific issues.

Time Frame:

It takes 15 to 40 minutes to complete a microlab, less time for groups of three addressing two to three questions, and more time for groups of four to five addressing four questions. Allow time for the whole group to debrief at the end.

Microlab Guidelines

1. Procedures:

All groups should consist of three to five people and be about the same size. It helps if people can pull chairs into a tight private group. The following techniques can be used to divide participants:

- Use cards with numbers on them, such as three 1s, 2s, and so on. If the numbers come out uneven, avoid groups of five. Make two groups of four instead.
- Count off by three.
- Group by level or category, including leading, learning, or problem-solving style.

2. Directions for Leader:

I'll be directing what we're going to be sharing. It's not an open discussion. It involves listening and sharing nonjudgmentally. I will pose one question at a time. Each person gets approximately 1 minute to answer it in turn. No one else is to talk or ask questions when it is someone else's turn. The goal is active listening. I will use a timer and tell the group when they should be halfway around. I also will tell you when the time is up for that question and what the next question is. If a person gets shortchanged on time for some reason, he or she can go first in the next round. The aim is to be open and honest and also to respect confidentiality. What someone says in your group is not to be repeated by anybody else. Can you agree to that?

3. Group Guidelines:

- Speak from your own experience. Say "I" when speaking about yourself.
- Stay on the suggested topic.
- Listen and discover rather than give advice.
- Avoid being judgmental.
- Respect shared confidences.
- It is okay to pass.

4. Debrief at the End:

The whole group should discuss the following: What do we now know about each other's ideas or experiences? Commonalities? Differences? What was helpful or positive about the process? What was difficult? Is it something to revisit in our work? How could you use the process in your work?

Descriptive Review

Purpose:

To reflect collaboratively on problems an individual or group brings to the table.

Time Frame:

Approximately 30 to 45 minutes.

Procedure:

1. The presenter describes the situation, providing as much information as possible about the context and the situation. If the situation involves other participants, they can add clarifying information.

2. The facilitator describes and summarizes the presenter's focusing question, for example: How can I get special needs students in my first period class to arrive on time?

3. The facilitator asks participants to ask clarifying questions. The questions go in the order of seating (preferably in a circle), one question per participant. Participants can pass if they do not have any questions. No one comments on any questions. Participants can build upon previous questions. Be very careful not to ask questions with hidden solutions, for example: Is it possible to set up a phone chain to the students' homes? The questions continue in order until no one needs more clarification.

4. The facilitator summarizes the proceedings thus far without making judgments and restates the focusing question.

5. The facilitator asks participants to make recommendations— again, in order, one recommendation at a time, and participants can build on previous recommendations. The facilitator takes notes on the recommendations. As always, participants can pass, and no comments are made about the recommendations.

6. When no new ideas remain, the facilitator summarizes the key points of the process and the main themes of the recommendations.

7. The presenter takes the notes and the facilitator requests that they reconvene in a month or so to see what decision the presenter made and the results of the decision.

8. The group debriefs the process and reflects on the positive aspects and makes suggestions for future Descriptive Reviews.

Vignette

To understand the versatility of the modified Descriptive Review, we will relate what happened to one of the authors in a post-master's leadership class.

One day, a skeptical student, who tended to mutter in the rear of the class, arrived somewhat more frazzled than usual. At one point during the class, she proclaimed that the leadership program did not deal with the real issues teachers and leaders had to confront. I asked her what was prompting her to make the comment. She responded that she was teaching a high school special education class at 8 o'clock in the morning and that she could not figure out how to get the students to arrive on time for class. She was at her wit's end, and furthermore, the administration was of no help.

I decided that her dilemma was a perfect opportunity to teach a modified form of Descriptive Review. The class was already seated in a semicircle. I acted as facilitator and asked her to state the problem as a focus question and to clarify the situation as much as possible. After the class asked more clarifying questions, the students began making recommendations. What is often remarkable about the Descriptive Review process is that the recommendations tend to build on each other and result in a few rich ideas. At the end of the recommendations and the summarizing of the main ideas and recommendations, the leadership candidate seemed less tense for the first time since she began attending the class.

The next week, she arrived at class almost bursting with excitement. She had not implemented any of our recommendations, but the process had inspired her. She had decided to use the process with her class to clarify why they were not getting to class on time and to solicit solutions from them. It had worked spectacularly. She now understood some of their barriers, and they had offered their own suggestions, which would promote their buy-in.

This example, which has been repeated in other venues (e.g., one of the authors working with new principal mentors who then used it with their mentees who then used it with their school staffs who then used it with their students), reinforces our contention that most of the practices we present are adaptable to almost any audience.

Site Practice: All Adults, Adaptable for Children

Choose a decision-making group with which you are involved. Ask permission to guide the group through the Descriptive Review Process to resolve a problem the group or an individual is facing. Take notes on what worked in the process and how you would handle it differently with the same or another group. Try and adapt it to your classroom for either a classroom management challenge or for a hands-on application. Compare the two processes. Share the results and your analysis with the class.

Small-Group Consultancies

When David Allen and Joe McDonald were at the Coalition of Essential Schools (Cushman, 1996), they developed "tuning protocols," that is, guides to looking collaboratively at student work. They adapted these techniques for the examination of larger school questions. We have also refined these processes in our work with groups, as have other facilitators (McDonald, Mohr, Dichter, & McDonald, 2003). The protocol we present is called "Small-Group Consultancies." As with most of the other problem-solving approaches, it can be used with any group of adults and with children, in this case most effectively with older ones. Similar to the descriptive review, this tool provides the opportunity for the presenter to receive feedback on the problem presented and the chance to reflect on the feedback. What is unique about this process is the possibility for the presenter to listen from the outside, without interruption and from different perspectives, to a discussion about the problem he or she has presented.

Vignette

The first time one of the authors used this process was in a somewhat risky situation. She was facilitating a retreat for a group of high school principals, most of them experienced and settled in their ways of dealing with concerns. The retreat was supposed to set the tone for relations with a recently appointed superintendent and for improvement for at-risk students in a school district where their needs were not being met. How could the author get the principals to listen to each other without interrupting and begin to address achievement problems? The unique setting of a retreat that permits reflection determined the decision to try the small-group consultancy. One principal volunteered to facilitate the small-group consultancy and another to present a problem. The highly structured process allowed for equal participation (difficult in a group of principals where each one is used to leading) and the initial thinking about a problem common to most of the principals involved. The tight structure permitted uncensored feedback and suggestions and encouraged other principals to reveal how they had or had not resolved the same problem. It also avoided the perennial problem of bragging and complaining.

Small-Group Consultancies

Purpose:

To obtain and reflect on direct and respectful feedback related to problems presented. To observe and reflect on this feedback from the outside.

Time Frame:

Approximately 40 to 60 minutes; time divisions are strictly kept.

Procedure:

1. *Introduction:* Facilitator explains the process and distributes steps, noting that the participants are to focus on the presenter's problem and not give examples of their own; the goal is to understand the problem thoroughly, not to give immediate solutions. The facilitator suggests the use of the phrase, "What I hear being said . . ." instead of "What I think should be done . . ." which can facilitate understanding.

2. *Presentation:* Presenter gives an overview of the issue or problem. The presenter may highlight specific questions or dilemmas related to the issue and may even share clarifying documents. Participants do not speak (7 to 10 minutes).

3. *Feedback:* Participants discuss what they have heard. Presenter listens, does not speak, takes notes, and highlights feedback that he or she wants to pursue. We recommend providing feedback in this order:

    -   WARM feedback: Respondents emphasize the strengths of the presenter's views and approaches to resolving the issue or problem.
    -   COOL feedback: Participants discuss dilemmas they heard or approaches they find problematic. Primarily, they pose questions about areas under question to encourage clarification and an expanded view of the problem and its possible solutions.

4. *Reflection:* The presenter reflects on both the warm and cool feedback. The goal is for the presenter to expand his or her thinking and to talk about how this has developed, not to respond to questions and reactions. The respondents listen without reacting.

5. *Conversation:* At this point, the presenter and respondents discuss and reflect together in an open conversation.

6. *Debriefing:* The presenter first reflects on how the process worked for him or her. The respondents then join in the debriefing. The participants think about how they can apply this process in other situations and in the classroom.

Site Practice: All Adults, Adaptable for Older Children

Ask permission to guide a group through the Small-Group Consultancy process to resolve a problem the group or an individual is facing. Take notes on what worked in the process and how you would handle it differently with the same or another group. Try to adapt it to a classroom of older children for either an academic or management challenge or for simulation of a content area discussion; for example, science, literature, or history would work well. Compare the two processes. Share the results and your analysis with the class.

Corporate Techniques

Pieces of the Pie

This tool is one of the easiest and most effective techniques to use when people need to understand different perspectives of a question. Dividing up a figurative pie according to the players involved in an issue or task (add a real pie to lighten up the task) allows the participants to actually "see" the various perspectives. This exercise can be used in any adult group or adapted for classroom use from elementary school through graduate school. It is particularly effective for school meetings where the various and varied stakeholders' perspectives need to be taken into consideration, even if they are not all at the table. This exercise has been adapted from *The Fifth Discipline Fieldbook* (Senge, Kleiner, Roberts, Ross, & Smith, 1994). We will present a model similar to the one in *The Fifth Discipline Fieldbook* and describe a variation that we have created.

Variation

When time is of the essence, Pieces of the Pie can be simplified by asking each participant to assume the role of one stakeholder. Each person presents one stakeholder's perspective. The rest of the process remains the same.

Example

One of the authors was unable to teach one of her class sessions and did not want to cancel the class. She asked for a class volunteer to facilitate the exercise and told the students to bring in a school

Pieces of the Pie

Purpose:

To provide the opportunity for a group to learn about and understand the different stakeholders' perspectives on an issue or problem. To broaden and deepen the understanding of the issue/problem and the possible consequences of various solutions.

Time Frame:

From 25 to 50 minutes.

Procedure:

1. Create the pie. Draw a large pie on chart paper. Cut into as many pieces as there are group members. If there are more than eight participants, divide into two groups. Write each person's name on a slice of the pie. Write the identified problem or an abbreviation or symbol for it at the center. Cut out the pie.

2. Use cards or strips of paper to write down each category of stakeholder, for example, teacher, student, parent, union representative, principal, superintendent. Place a card at the edge of each piece of pie. Then post a sheet of chart paper for each stakeholder.

3. The pie is then placed so each named person has a stakeholder card next to his or her name. Each person then writes something about the problem on the appropriate flip chart from his or her stakeholder's point of view. Comments may raise questions or offer solutions but must be from the point of view of the stakeholder. It is important to try to reflect on and see what is unique to that stakeholder's perspective. What data and knowledge influence that particular perspective?

4. Once each person has posted a comment (no passing), the pie is turned, and everyone takes another stakeholder's perspective. The cycle continues until all participants have taken all perspectives.

5. Once the cycle has been completed, the group can talk through the issue or problem from each description. The next step will be problem solving.

problem. When the author returned the next week, a problem had been clarified and recommendations offered. The student had wanted to look at the new special education continuum and the implementation problems the school was having. It was an ideal problem to analyze because of the large, very involved group of stakeholders. The whole process was recorded on chart paper, and the student whose problem had been chosen asked to bring the results back to her school to share with her school's leadership team. The principal role of leadership in this example was empowering the leadership candidates—one of the most crucial lessons of leadership.

Rating and Ranking

These techniques are visual, clear, and about as objective as problem-solving tools can be. They allow a group to compare and evaluate a list of possible solutions against a set of guidelines. The factual basis for some possible guidelines, for example, cost, time, and so on, can advance reaching a decision. The "Catch-22" is choosing appropriate guidelines. Many teachers and administrators rank this tool as one of their favorites because of the aforementioned reasons. Rating gives a "score" to decision-making guidelines, and ranking scores the alternatives against each other. They can be used as a follow-up to some of the more reflective brainstorming tools, for example, Descriptive Review, Small-Group Consultancy, and so on. We present completed tables to clarify how the process works (see Tables 7.1 and 7.2).

Table 7.1   Rating Guidelines

Alternatives	Cost	Time	Acceptability	Authorization	Efficacy	Total
Increase parent involvement	1 = low 10 = high	1 = short 10 = long	1 = high 10 = low	1 = easy 10 = hard	1 = high 10 = low	
Monthly newsletter	2	3	2	1	8	**16**
Home visits	6	7	6	7	2	**28**
Adult courses	4	5	2	2	3	**16**
Babysitting for PTA, parent conferences	4	3	2	4	5	**18**
Monthly award ceremonies	2	4	2	5	6	**19**

Table 7.2   Ranking Guidelines

Alternatives	Cost	Time	Acceptability	Authorization	Efficacy	Total
Increase parent involvement	1–5	1–5	1–5	1–5	1–5	
Monthly newsletter	1	1	1	1	5	**9**
Home visits	5	5	5	5	1	**21**
Adult courses	4	4	2	2	2	**14**
Babysitting for PTA, parent conferences	2	2	4	3	3	**14**
Monthly award ceremonies	3	3	3	4	4	**17**

Rating and Ranking

Purpose:

To evaluate and compare a list of possible solutions against a set of guidelines.

Time Frame:

From 25 to 50 minutes.

Procedure:

1. Determine the guidelines the solution must meet. Guidelines vary according to the problem or issue. Brainstorm questions about the solution. Narrow the list to those you need to answer to solve the problem. Then, choose the three to five most important guidelines (Nominal Group Process works well for this task).

2. Create a numerical score for each guideline, making sure the scales run the same way for all guidelines. If a guideline is more important, it can be weighted by multiplying it by 2. Do not forget that guidelines and their importance vary from site to site, in time, and so on. If you are ranking your alternatives against each other, assign a "1" for the best, a "2" for the next best, and so on. Repeat for each guideline.

3. Tabulate the score for each alternative. Common sense may reveal that the winning alternative is not the best. In that case, reexamine the guidelines.

Force Field Analysis

Before making decisions on how to resolve an issue, a group usually needs to look at the causes of a problem and to get a sense of the larger picture. Force Field Analysis allows a group (of any type or age) to represent graphically the positive and negative forces that can impede or support reaching a goal (see Figure 7.1). It also helps determine graphically which forces are the most powerful. This tool is effective with the whole range of adult groups in a school and can serve as a graphic organizer in the classroom. Imagine using it in a social studies class: The students can analyze graphically the positive and negative origins of a war.

Force Field Analysis

Purpose:

To describe and analyze graphically the positive forces that could move the group toward a goal and those that are preventing the group from achieving its goal.

Time Frame:

From 20 to 30 minutes.

Procedure:

1. Clearly identify the goal the group is trying to achieve or the problem to be resolved.

2. Draw a solid line across a chart, and label it with the goal.

3. List the forces that are moving or could move you toward your goal. These forces should be written on the arrows pointing up toward the line.

4. List the restraining forces, those that are and/or will keep the group from reaching its goal or solving the problem.

5. Examine both the positive and negative forces, and decide which ones in each category are the strongest. The group can then begin problem-solving strategies to encourage the positive forces and minimize the negative ones.

Figure 7.1   Force Field Analysis

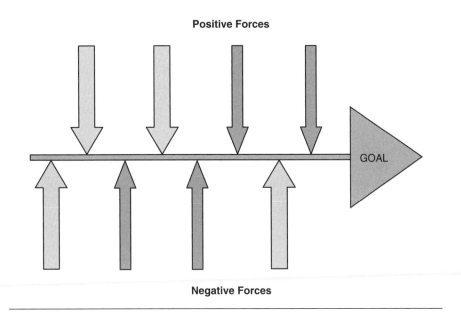

Vignette

A few years ago, several leadership candidates in an internship group with which one of the authors was working came to class very frustrated. The interns had found the school leaders with whom they were working to be less than exemplary. How were they to learn to become effective leaders in a dysfunctional environment? I immediately realized that I had to turn the situation into a productive one and decided to use the situation as a double "teachable moment," demonstrating how to make a potential gripe session into a positive experience and modeling an effective strategy for this transformation. I chose the Force Field Analysis for this situation because the discontented participants could share their frustrations and see them validated. A structured process where people can voice dissatisfaction without changing the tone and purpose of a meeting is one of the most valuable leadership tools. The goal the interns chose was how to get the most out of the internship experience. Figure 7.2 displays their findings.

The Fishbone

The Fishbone diagram enables a group to systematically analyze the causes of a problem or the consequences of proposed solutions. The visual display helps organize and expand thinking (see Figure 7.3).

Figure 7.2   Force Field Analysis in Practice

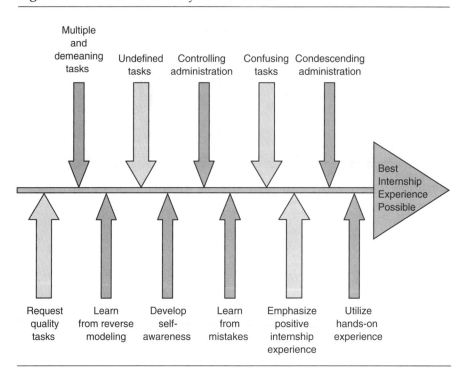

There are variations of the Fishbone diagram. We are limiting our suggestions to the basic Fishbone and a suggestion for promoting wider input in a school environment.

Bulletin Board Fishbone

Once participants are familiar with the Fishbone process, a diagram can be posted in the teachers' room, parents' room, and in the hallway. The box is drawn with the description of the identified problem, and one long arrow is drawn. Post-its and writing implements are placed next to it, and members of the group contribute to the Fishbone. This strategy can save a lot of meeting time and involve some people who might not otherwise participate.

Example

A Brooklyn, New York, middle school held a two-day retreat that some teachers could not attend. Significant initiatives and problems were discussed and in some cases resolved at the retreat. To foster the buy-in of the staff members who were not involved, the retreat leaders drew Fishbone diagrams of the major issues and posted them

---

The Fishbone

Purpose:

To provide a visual display of the major contributing categories of causes and their components to a problem.

Time Frame:

From 20 to 30 minutes.

Procedure:

1. Clearly identify the problem to be analyzed.

2. Write a summary statement of the problem in a box. Draw a long arrow across the chart that reaches the box.

3. Determine the main categories of the causes of the problem, and draw the "bones" of the fish to represent them. Think of different types of categories (e.g., Figure 7.3—People, Resources, Environment, and Curriculum), but limit the number of categories (3–5).

4. Break down the causes into smaller components, or subcategories (e.g., Figure 7.3—under "People," Parents, Teachers, Children, and Administrators).

5. Determine specific contributing factors within each subcategory.

6. The next step will be to problem solve the categories that have been clearly identified.

---

on prominently situated bulletin boards. Post-its and pens were attached, and the school community was encouraged to include additional input. The issues resolved were enriched, and the remaining issues received a fresh influx of ideas. The posting of the Fishbone and similar graphics became an integral part of the meeting process, opening and deepening the school community dialogue.

Double Reversal

When a team is in a rut, this technique allows new ideas to emerge and encourages "out-of-the-box" thinking. It also can be a lot of fun and restore good humor to a frustrated group (see Table 7.3).

Figure 7.3 Fishbone Diagram

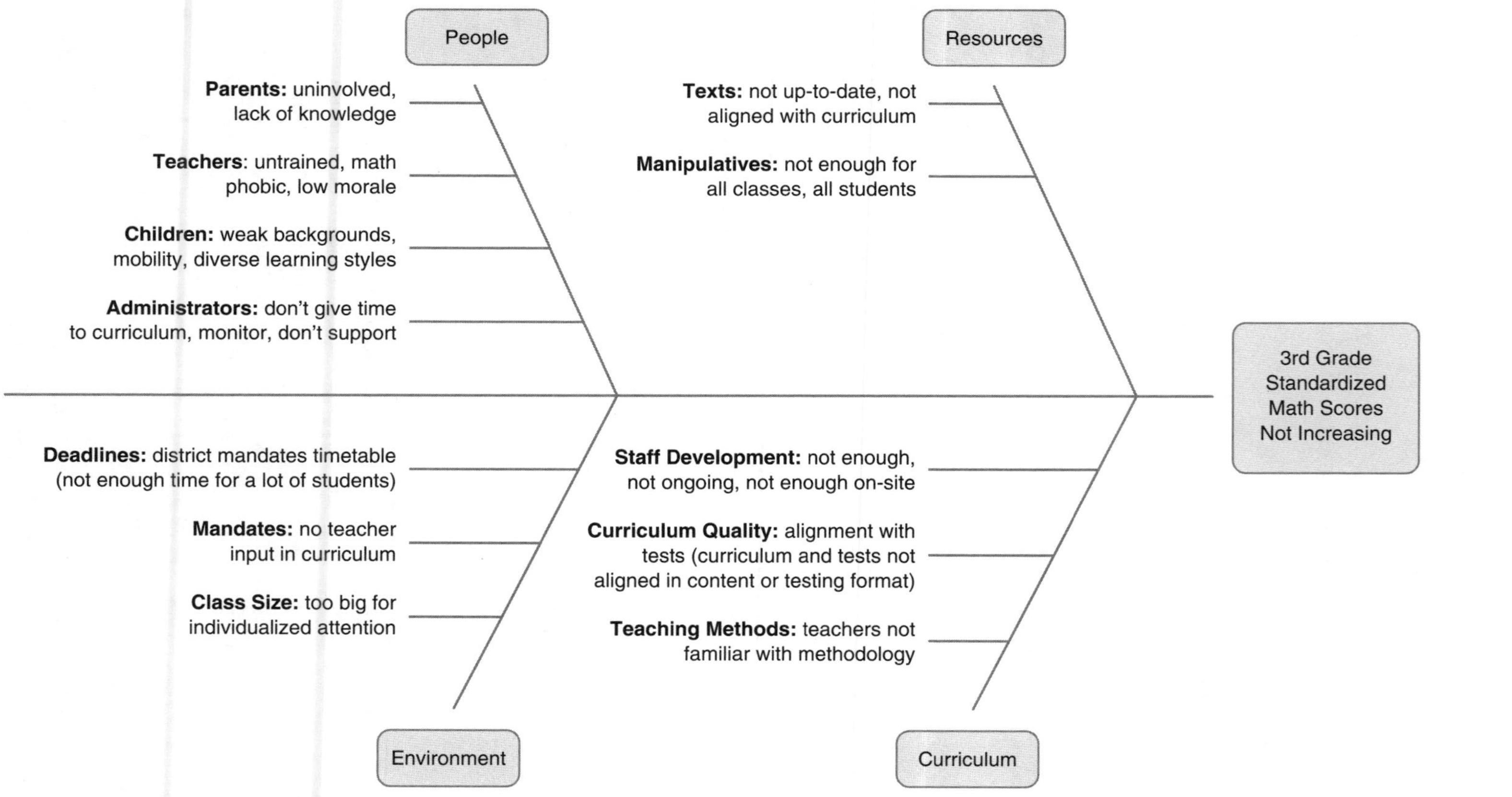

Resources

Texts: not up-to-date, not aligned with curriculum

Manipulatives: not enough for all classes, all students

People

Parents: uninvolved, lack of knowledge

Teachers: untrained, math phobic, low morale

Children: weak backgrounds, mobility, diverse learning styles

Administrators: don't give time to curriculum, monitor, don't support

3rd Grade Standardized Math Scores Not Increasing

Staff Development: not enough, not ongoing, not enough on-site

Curriculum Quality: alignment with tests (curriculum and tests not aligned in content or testing format)

Teaching Methods: teachers not familiar with methodology

Curriculum

Environment

Deadlines: district mandates timetable (not enough time for a lot of students)

Mandates: no teacher input in curriculum

Class Size: too big for individualized attention

Double Reversal

Purpose:

To provide a visual display of the major contributing categories of causes and their components to a problem.

Time Frame:

From 20 to 30 minutes.

Procedure:

1. List the goals your problem is preventing you from achieving.
2. Reverse the goals.
3. List all the ideas you can think of to achieve each reversed goal.
4. Reverse each "reversed" idea.
5. Incorporate the new ideas into another problem-solving process.

Example

High teacher turnover in an elementary school is preventing the achievement of the following goals: (a) a cohesive, collaborative faculty and (b) a shared knowledge base, methodological foundation, and vocabulary for teaching and learning.

Chapter Summary

The purpose of this chapter was to provide a variety of strategies, techniques, and exercises that exemplify collaborative, constructivist, and reflective principles. We could fill an entire book with different processes. Our choices are based on what has worked for us and is appropriate for school environments. Our suggested readings, applicable to Chapters 5 through 7, include books that offer more examples based on our guiding principles. Chapter 8 concludes our book with a case study that is a composite of experiences we have observed and in which we have participated. The study pulls together many of the ideas and practices we recommend and can serve as a model of "walking the talk": transforming espoused theories into theories-in-use.

Table 7.3   Double Reversal: Teacher Turnover

Goal: Low teacher turnover	Reversed Goal: High teacher turnover
a. Cohesive, collaborative faculty	a. Divided, isolated faculty
b. Shared knowledge base, methodological foundation, and vocabulary for teaching and learning	b. "Sink or swim" in teaching and learning

Strategies for Reversed Goals	Reversal of Reversed Strategies
a. Divided isolated faculty	a. Cohesive, collaborative faculty
• Hold few meetings and only in big groups • Conduct meetings autocratically • Do not schedule common planning time • Single out faculty who accomplish required tasks • Post lists of faculty who have not completed tasks	• Hold frequent, small-group meetings • Plan and conduct meetings collaboratively • Schedule frequent common planning time • Recognize many faculty for varied accomplishments • Work behind the scenes with staff that need support
b. "Sink or swim" in teaching and learning	b. Shared knowledge base
• No professional development • No mentoring • No intervisitation of classes • No professional library • Constant monitoring and evaluation	• Frequent, ongoing professional development • Create mentoring plan for novice faculty and peer coaching for rest • Class intervisitations as part of mentoring, peer coaching, and professional development • Creation of professional library • Observations with the goal of support and improvement of instruction

Notes

1. Courtesy of Daniel Barron, National School Reform Faculty.

2. We thank Emily White of Bank Street College of Education and Linda Lantieri of Educators for Social Responsibility for allowing us to adapt their guidelines.

Suggested Readings

Beebe, S. A., & Masterson, J. T. (2000). *Communicating in small groups* (6th ed.). New York: Longman.

Doyle, M., & Straus, D. (1982). *How to make meetings work.* New York: Jove Books.

McDonald, J. P., Mohr, N., Dichter, A., & McDonald, E. C. (2003). *The power of protocols.* New York: Teachers College Press.

Roberts, S. & Pruitt, E. (2003). *Schools as professional learning communities.* Thousand Oaks, CA: Corwin.

Senge, P. M. (1990). *The fifth discipline: The art and practice of the learning organization.* New York: Doubleday.

Senge, P. M., Cambron-McCabe, N., Lucas, T., Smith, B., Dutton, J., & Kleiner, A. (2000). *Schools that learn: The fifth discipline fieldbook for educators, parents, and everyone who cares about education.* New York: Doubleday-Currency.

Senge, P., Kleiner, A., Roberts, C., Ross, R. B., & Smith, B. (1994). *A fifth discipline fieldbook for educators, parents, and everyone who cares about education.* New York: Doubleday.

Straus, D. (2002). *How to make collaboration work: Powerful ways to build consensus, solve problems, and make decisions.* San Francisco: Berret-Koehler.

Woolfolk, A., & Hoy, W. K. (2003). *Instructional leadership: A learning-centered guide.* Boston: Allyn & Bacon.

8

Pulling It Together

Understanding that a sense of community strongly influences student development, educational leaders must focus their attention on activities that enhance the sense of community within the school.

—Quick and Normore (2004, p. 338)

Case Study: Fieldston Middle School, Burlington School District, Anywhere, USA

Community of Learners in Practice: Challenges and Opportunities

The location and names of participants are fictitious, but we believe the following case represents the realities of establishing and maintaining an educational learning community, with all its difficulties and prospects, to ensure high achievement for all children. Obviously, the case we present does not represent every attempt to establish a learning community. The events and circumstances in the school and district are unique. No quick and easy recipes for success are available for anything, let alone establishing learning communities. The nature of leadership and supervision is highly contextual. This case and its descriptions are idiosyncratic but do reveal some of the challenges and opportunities you may face in the attempt to lead organizational and school reform.

Read the case and, most important, discuss the reflective questions that follow.

Setting: A Vision of a New Superintendent

Fieldston Middle School is not atypical of the two middle schools, one high school, and five elementary schools in Burlington, Anywhere, USA. In fact, Fieldston Middle School is beset by some of the same conditions found in many schools in the state. In a report issued by the Governor's Commission on School Improvement published last week, the following summary findings on the Fieldston Middle School in Burlington are striking:

- Significant and widespread declines in academic achievement
- Lack of curriculum renewal
- Evaluation, not supervision that promotes good teaching, is the focus
- Less family involvement in schools
- Decreasing teacher satisfaction and morale
- Increasing reports of student misbehavior, truancy, and gang involvement
- Low levels of positive school climate as assessed by question-naires collected from students, parents, teachers, and even school administrators
- High levels of administrator turnover and high rates of teacher attrition

At a recent school board meeting late in the school year, Rajat Kumar, parent activist, vociferously criticized the board for its inaction and indecision in terms of offering proposals for school renewal. "Any of us," explained Mr. Kumar, "who has visited Fieldston over the past few years can attest to the disarray that pervades the school. . . . I mean the lack of clear and compelling vision for school improvement, leaders and some teachers without commitment to do whatever it takes to raise student achievement. . . . I can go on. But it's not only their fault, it's ours as well. Where are the resources, financial, personnel and otherwise, that are necessary to turn our school around? Where have we been? What are we doing? What are we going to do?" Echoing his dissatisfaction, Samantha Lui, a parent of a sixth grader at Fieldston, decried the pervasive "bad politics" that "have characterized our school district for too long." "We don't really care about the children . . . we care about our personal vested

interests . . . all the infighting nauseates me . . . we're interested only
in our own point of view. We don't really listen to each other, let alone
trust and respect each other. It's time we took the proverbial 'bull by
the horn' and did something to ensure that not only Fieldston in
particular but all our schools are models of high achievement for all
students in the district and the state. Yes, what are we going to do?"

"What can we do?" shouted Christia Youssef from the audience,
seated near the rear of the full school auditorium. "With no superintendent [Mr. Christopher Eagleton recently resigned to assume a
superintendency in the Northeast], what can we do? It seems to me
the first thing we must do is find a leader with vision and then provide him or her with the resources and means to get the job done
to turn our schools around." Applause filled the crowded standing-
room-only auditorium.

Continued heated discussions lead to the formation of a district
subcommittee of school board members along with three teachers,
two school administrators, two students, five parent volunteers not
seated on the board, and a fairly popular local politician to meet to
develop a strategic proposal for school renewal. The committee
worked many long hours over the final month of the school year.
Although the committee could not decide on an educational vision or
course of action to turn around the schools, committee members did
create a search protocol for a new superintendent. Within 6 weeks, the
board unanimously hired a new superintendent. Joshua Ye, subcommittee chair, marveled at how they were able to come together in a
relatively short period of time without too much dissent and recommend a superintendent candidate for full school board approval.
"Miracles are still possible," he chuckled at a board meeting. "But the
real hard work lies ahead."

The successful candidate impressed the subcommittee and board
with her determination, vision, and unusual request, at least unusual
for the Burlington School District. She requested as follows: "Hire a
superintendent you trust, and give the person the resources needed
to turn around the schools and, first and foremost, reform practices at
the district level. District management and leadership here have been
abysmal, by your own admission. District leaders, including board
members, need to work as a team. It doesn't mean we'll agree all the
time. In fact, we'll agree not to agree many times. But the point is we
need a unified vision and commitment . . . and it must begin at the
top. We cannot expect any school to follow suit unless we present a
model of leadership that is valued and respected. Now, if that candidate is me, I want carte blanche, within reason, to do what I believe

will create the best learning environment for the boys and girls of this district, who deserve only the best. All I ask for is patience, because I have no panaceas, but I will help construct, build a vision of possibility, of hope . . . a hope for a better future, a better education, a better school system that all stakeholders—I mean teachers, administrators, parents, students, and community leaders—can be proud of. Why? Because we will all have a vested interest in its success, because we will all be involved as a community, a community of learners in which each person is valued and supported. Together, we can build a school that prides itself on high achievement for all students and establish rigorous standards for achievement—but also be equally concerned about nurturing in our students caring, thoughtful, civic-minded individuals who value respect and hard work. Our schools must educate *all* children and youth to act responsibly as citizens who live with pride in a social and political democracy."

Underlying Principles: Constructivism and Reflective Practice

Michelle Carroll became superintendent of the Burlington School District. Never before had the district and board unanimously supported a candidate. She was a take-charge, visionary leader (a "Dynamic Assertive," of course—remember Chapter 2?) who was committed to "revitalizing" the district. Charged by the board specifically to improve reading and math scores and raise achievement levels across the curriculum, the new district superintendent, conversant with current literature in the field, decided to put together a leadership team to spearhead reform efforts at the district level first. Dr. Carroll's goal was to build a learning community by developing and nurturing connections between people, socially and intellectually, at all levels in the district. At a staff meeting, she explained, "Building a learning community is tantamount to developing a commitment to shared learning." "Together," she continued, "we must be willing to learn and grow together. A problem doesn't exist for me, but must be viewed as a shared obligation . . . how can *we* better understand the situation and resolve together to develop strategies, if not solutions?!"

Dr. Carroll openly shared her belief and commitment to constructivism and reflective practice. She was a hands-on educator who believed every good theory had a practical base, as practice itself was grounded in theory. "Frame an idea, a theory," she was fond of saying, "but always find or create it in the lived experiences of practitioners." With Dewey and Vygotsky as her mentors, she put her words into action, always challenging others to construct meaning on their own by always applying theory to the world of practice.

The superintendent also explained her commitment to reflective practice: "Reflection is the heart of professional practice. Reflective practice is a process by which you take the time to contemplate and assess the efficacy of programs and practices in order to determine their appropriateness or effectiveness so that improvements or refinements might be achieved. Research-oriented educators are engaged in ongoing self-study in which they assess the needs of their classrooms and schools, identify problem areas, and develop strategies for becoming more effective." She realized, though, that instilling habits of reflection, critical inquiry, and training in reflection is not always easy. She challenged her hand-picked staff to ask these questions:

1. What concerns us?

2. Why are we concerned?

3. Can we confirm our perceptions?

4. What mistakes have we made?

5. If we were able to do it again, what would we do differently?

6. What are our current options?

7. What evidence can we collect to confirm our feelings?

8. Who might be willing to share their ideas with us?

9. What have our successes been?

10. How might we replicate these successes?

11. In what other ways might we improve our work in the district, school, and classroom?

Dr. Carroll explained further that "our work is riddled with situations that demand quick action and almost immediate response. We must still stay the course." Quoting the work of Donald Schon (1983, 1984, 1987), who advocates reflection in and on the practice of education, she continued, "Schon maintains that 'the problems of real-world practice do not present themselves as problems at all but as messy, indeterminate situations' (1987, p. 4). Schon (1987) describes two types of reflective thinking: *reflection-in-action* and *reflection-on-action*. Reflection-in-action is the ability to 'think on one's feet' when faced with the many surprises and challenges in our daily lives in schools. You are able to 'think on your feet' as you face the multitude of crises that are all too common in almost any district, classroom, or school. You must often decide quickly when confronted by an irate parent's demand that she be allowed 'to whip' her child in front of the class. Even when challenged by less inflammatory situations, you must act decisively.

"On the other hand, Schon also discusses reflection-on-action, which is most relevant to our work at the district level. Reflection-on-action occurs when educators look back upon their work and consider what practices were successful and what areas need improvement. Reflection-on-action is critical to understanding and thinking about events and phenomena as they unfold in the district, classroom, and school. Special time must be set aside to allow for reflection-on-action.

"I realize that we are all overwhelmed and sometimes incapable of dealing with increased demands, and we think that reflection-on-action is impossible when, in fact, it is not only essential, but indeed possible. How, then, can we find the time to become a 'reflective educator'? Here is a suggestion I'll ask each and every one of us to try: Set aside 15 to 30 minutes a day for reflective thinking. Build time into your schedule by closing your office door for 20 minutes so you are not disturbed. During this isolated time, deliberate on the overall structure of the day or on one specific issue we are tackling. Ask, 'What can I contribute? What can we do?'

"Moreover, I am instituting a 'cabinet meeting' every day, from 7:30 a.m. until around 9:00 a.m., before things get too hectic around here. Such meetings will allow supervisory personnel to 'reflect' and bring up important issues for general discussion. Anyone on the staff is allowed to attend these meetings to share their concerns or simply join in on 'reflecting.'"

Dr. Carroll concluded her meeting by explaining, "One of the most important decisions you must make is whether or not to become a 'reflective practitioner.' A reflective educator is someone who takes the time to think about what has transpired or what steps should be taken tomorrow. Reflective educators think before they act. They are proactive, not reactive. Reflective educators care enough about their jobs to take the time to consider what works and what doesn't."

Prerequisites: Leadership, Communication, and Vision

Dr. Carroll also realized the importance of self-knowledge for those engaged in leadership activities. "Awareness of our identity helps determine how we understand and practice leadership and engage in relationships that are integral to it. Knowledge of our strengths and weaknesses, our personality preferences, what drives and motivates us, and the impact we have on others can influence our actions." She employed the personal "Leadership Styles Inventory" described in Chapter 2 to select and reposition her leadership team. She then gathered the team. They took the inventory and discussed the results among themselves. She asked, "Do the inventory results match your personal assessment of your leadership style?" "What evidence can you cite to support your position?" In small groups, she asked each leader to share his or her inventory results. Each leader was expected to raise points that might either confirm or question personal observations. Each leader later met with Dr. Carroll to discuss which precise leadership position would make the most sense given one's leadership style, abilities, and interests. Although the superintendent did attract some new faces to the district, she purposely wanted to utilize the talent that already existed but refocus their work based upon personal strengths and unique leadership styles, believing that leadership exists in all individuals. Her willingness to listen, share, and lead with compassion in a very short time earned her a sterling reputation from the very start.

Dr. Carroll realized that communication networks throughout the district had decayed to the point that little, if any, information was communicated in a meaningful way. She was aware that communication must begin at the top. She engaged her staff in some of the techniques described in Chapter 3. She practiced these listening and communicating skills with her staff not just through lecture, but through lived experience. Staff appreciated the fact that "Michelle 'walks the talk.'" She also used the "Learning Connections Inventory" discussed in Chapter 3. She aimed to help leaders uncover their personal learning preferences or inclinations. The activity helped to bond the group and develop important social skills needed for school leadership. Dr. Carroll decided to divide participants into groups after they had taken the inventory. After intense and guided sharing, she facilitated whole-group discussion to highlight important insights and lessons of the experience. Later, she met with each individual on a voluntary basis to discuss private reactions and insights. She helped each individual draw implications for his or her own work in schools.

Superintendent Carroll also challenged her supervisory staff to develop a personal vision statement not unlike the one described in Chapter 4. She led her team through the exercise, and then during a weekend retreat at her beachfront home, they shared their vision statements and spent much time aligning their statements so that some sort of unifying theme emerged that would benefit the district as a whole. Yearly objectives emerged from the themes, and a course of action was planned along with a systematic assessment plan.

Equipped with personal understanding of who they were as leaders and learners and how that knowledge was reflected in their collective leadership vision, they were then prepared to tackle the skills needed to lead and participate in groups and teams. Under Dr. Carroll's patient guidance, they practiced the skills and strategies essential for effective meetings and other social interactions. They also practiced the listening and other communication skills addressed in Chapter 5 of this book. Dr. Carroll fully realized that many of the problems the district previously encountered stemmed from not merely a lack of communication, but from personal and interpersonal interactions that served as barriers to effective communication. At one of her 3-day retreats, she incorporated icebreakers, had the teams develop ground rules that set the tone for enhancing communication, and drew on problem-solving strategies to resolve issues.

At one session, Dr. Carroll used the Descriptive Review. She asked for a volunteer to share a problem. Wendy Stevenson, a new elementary school principal, explained her difficulty in soliciting volunteers for her afterschool teacher leadership team. After confirming that others in the group considered this topic worthy of further explanation, the superintendent posed the question to the group, "How can we engender faculty interest to serve on voluntary schoolwide committees?" She then asked the group to ask clarifying questions. After some time, Dr. Carroll summarized the discussion and reviewed the questions, making sure not to take a stance or offer her opinion. She then asked participants to make recommendations. One middle school principal suggested that they might provide incentives to teachers to encourage greater participation. Another principal noted, perhaps more fundamentally, that they establish administrative and/or instructional support structures that would create a school atmosphere conducive to collaboration and volunteerism. After about 20 minutes, Dr. Carroll summarized the insights offered. She then recorded major themes that emerged from the discussion and encouraged participants to develop an action plan of sorts that included a variety of options. She informed the group that they would meet in a month's time to share implementation experiences of any of the participants. Members of the group felt supported because Dr. Carroll had created a learning environment that was nonthreatening and that encouraged risk taking. She was fond of saying, "There are no winners or losers. We are all committed to excellence, and that means trying new ideas, even if they don't work at first."

Gaining a Foothold: Start Small and Work Gradually

Dr. Carroll ensured that the skills gained from the retreats were modeled in everyday interactions in the district office and when working with school administrators. Her plan was to develop these skills among her team members and then to model and work with administrators and teachers at various school sites. She realized that these strategies only set the tone or established a milieu conducive to community building in schools. If such practices were to become commonplace in schools, then an overall plan had to be developed over time. She realized that lasting change occurs by degree, not decree. She purposely decided to start her ideas on a small scale and build from one small success after another. Her main focus then was on Fieldston Middle School, and not even the whole school. Rather, she'd focus her efforts on working with the building principal, assistant principal, and sixth-grade teachers. Once success was experienced, the groundswell for her ideas would be established, and success would grow almost by itself.

The Key to School Success: Focus on Instruction

Dr. Carroll realized that the only way to eventually raise student achievement was to focus on instructional leadership. She realized she needed to appoint individuals to principalships and assistant principalships who had a strong and deep-seated commitment to instructional improvement.

Past practices in the district, however, relied on hiring supervisors who were good managers but not necessarily effective instructional leaders. She realized that emerging trends in supervisory practice must emphasize (a) training for administrators as well as teachers in supervision, mentoring, and coaching; (b) sensitivity to the processes of professional growth and continuous improvement; (c) training in observation and reflection on practice; (d) integration of supervision with staff development, curriculum development, and school improvement systems; (e) collegial assistance among educators, parents, and students; and so on. In sum, she wanted leaders who believed that supervision of instruction must be collaborative, collegial, and democratic.

The Realities of Leadership: Leader Styles Are Critical

While Dr. Carroll was conversant with the literature on instructional improvement, she was equally conversant in the theories of natural leadership qualities and ethical virtues. Having read Chapter 2 of this book and understood the interrelationships among leadership qualities and the importance of leadership virtues, she was now ready to put these ideas into action. She knew that many educators may have the requisite knowledge and skills to enhance instructional leadership. But, she asked, "Are they in the right positions to be able to transform knowledge into action?" She understood that espousing a democratic and collaborative vision is very different from making it a reality. She also realized the political dimension required to transform a school or a district. She wanted leaders who not only understood this political dimension but also had the gumption (courage and imagination) to make the tough decisions that would be required.

Dr. Carroll was given authority, as she had requested upon hire, to appoint not only a cadre of leaders in the district office but also individuals into interim principalships. She developed a list of two dozen candidates who had reputations as strong instructional leaders with proven records of performance. Yet she realized that leadership is situational. An effective principal in one setting (e.g., an affluent neighborhood with multiple resources and a majority of untenured teachers) may be less so in another (e.g., an inner-city neighborhood with fewer resources and a majority of tenured teachers). Armed with the knowledge of leadership qualities, Dr. Carroll began to match individual strengths with situational requirements. Although certainly not an exact science, such an undertaking was guided by several key questions that she posed:

- What are the position vacancies (i.e., principal vacancies and positions in the district office)?
- What are the unique needs of each school (considering demographics, experience levels of teachers, achievement scores, current instructional programs, PTA membership, etc.)? What kind of team will she need in the district office to carry out her new instructional policies?
- What are the specific challenges in each school (e.g., is the school in disarray organizationally, does the school lack visionary leadership, or are teachers complacent and lack the motivation to try harder)? What is the "heart" of the problem that exists in a particular school?
- What are the unique strengths of each (principal and district leader) candidate?

Using the information in Chapter 2, Dr. Carroll identified characteristics she deemed necessary for each school. In fact, she made a grid
that identified each school and listed three major requirements that
would make it more effective. For example, School X had a sound
curriculum, sufficient instructional materials, and adequate "person-
power" but lacked a leader who could empower other leaders to form
a learning community. She then listed each principal candidate and
listed each one's major quality. School X, according to Dr. Carroll,
needed a Dynamic Assertive leader who could rock the boat and motivate the many to a collective vision. The candidate had to demonstrate,
above all else, the courage to make tough and right decisions that
would upset taken-for-granted practices and programs. No matter how
qualified Candidate X was with his years of excellent service and outstanding organizational skills, he would be the wrong leader in this
particular school. As an Adaptive Assertive, he would be better suited
in School Y, which needed someone who could coordinate and organize instructional activities in a more coherent fashion than had been
done in the past. In School Z, for instance, a Dynamic Supportive
leader who displayed, above all else, impartiality and empathy might
be a more effective leader than the aforementioned leaders.

As for her team in the district office, Dr. Carroll established goals
and objectives for each position and then matched the qualities to the
position. For example, she wanted a team member or two who were
expert instructional leaders, who could relate to teachers in a nonauthoritarian manner. She might decide, then, to select a Dynamic
Supportive or even an Adaptive Supportive individual to fill these
positions. On the other hand, she would need an individual to wade
through the politics and oppositions that inevitably arise in every
change effort. Therefore she knew she needed an Adaptive Aggressive
who would ensure, at all costs, that the vision would become a reality.

Above all, Dr. Carroll knew that she wanted leaders, not followers.
She wanted to empower her leadership team so that they, in turn,
would empower others. Developing a learning community where individual strengths of all educators were identified, valued, and nurtured
was central to her task. Effective leadership, for Carroll, relied on individuals of different qualities working together toward a shared goal.

A Rocky Start: The Case of Principal Rashid

Dr. Carroll selected Soffiyya Rashid as principal of Fieldston Middle
School. Ms. Rashid was a Dynamic Supportive whom the superintendent felt would nurture faculty and staff in nonauthoritarian,
nonautocratic ways, a sharp contrast with the former principal, who

ruled with "a tight fist" and ostracized many teachers and put others in fear. Although Ms. Rashid was eager, her battle was uphill. Fieldston reflected all of the problems previously mentioned in the Governor's Commission on School Improvement. The principal decided to take small steps over time, realizing that radical transformations were dangerous, if not lethal, to a school culture that was confused and immature. Teachers were apprehensive and distrustful. Parental involvement was nonexistent. The initial success Dr. Carroll experienced in establishing her leadership team at the district level would not be replicated at Fieldston School. Ms. Rashid encountered enormous opposition.

After sharing her vision and ideas about community building with sixth-grade teachers, Ms. Rashid received a lukewarm response. Skeptical of change regardless of how collegial and nonthreatening it was presented as being, teachers didn't volunteer to participate in the principal's plan. A hushed silence filled the room as she waited for volunteers or for someone to at least ask some questions.

Ms. Rashid then decided that some icebreaking activity was appropriate. She divided the group into two teams and used one of the activities described in Chapter 6. Although not much else was accomplished that day, at least teachers left the room a bit cheerful after partaking in the activity. They also had learned a little about each other, making a small dent in the teachers' feelings of isolation.

The principal decided to approach two of the sixth-grade teachers who had shown an inkling of interest during the previous session. "Would you mind assisting me in thinking through how we might reorganize or rethink how teaching and learning take place in this grade? It seems to me, and correct me if I'm mistaken, that teachers work in isolation from one another with little, if any, collaboration about curricular or instructional matters." She then shared her passion for constructivist thinking and reflective practice, which she had shared with Dr. Carroll. The teachers agreed to continue private conversations with the principal. Over the next several weeks, the two teachers met with Ms. Rashid to develop a vision of reform that excited them. Sharing ideas with one another was a fresh experience for both teachers, one that they appreciated. They began with a brainstorming exercise to jump-start their thinking. Then Ms. Rashid guided them through Force Field Analysis to narrow their new palette of ideas. The principal asked whether the teachers would mind presenting their ideas at the next grade conference. Initially reluctant, they finally consented.

Ms. Rashid began the meeting with the "Choosing Your Direction" exercise so the faculty could learn about their problem-solving orientations. Groups were then drawn up based on problem-solving styles. All the styles were represented in each group. The groups then used the Nominal Group Process to narrow down the ideas they wanted to include in their reform vision. The ideas chosen by the most groups became the basis of their vision.

Although a few teachers remained obstinate, others thought the ideas they heard sounded interesting. As the year progressed, the following was observed: Romi Shtricker, one of the grade leaders, was most enthusiastic. "You mean our principal will allow us to experiment by reorganizing our schedules to facilitate this 'team' concept?" Four teachers later got together to work out a team approach using interdisciplinary study for their classes. They volunteered to work with Ms. Rashid on their lunch and during their preps. They mentored each other, used peer-coaching strategies, and all the while received encouragement and support from their principal. Ms. Rashid was able to generate some financial resources with the support of Dr. Carroll, who was thrilled about the prospects of curriculum renewal at Fieldston, even though it was for just one grade, and only two classes at that.

Curriculum Renewal at Fieldston: The Beginnings of Community Learning

News spread fast at Fieldston. These teachers were more excited than they had been in years. They had even attended a series of workshops on action research. Ms. Rashid offered to withdraw the district policy of mandatory evaluation in the form of formal observations if they would apply their newfound action research strategies toward assessing the effectiveness of the curriculum program. Their infectious enthusiasm influenced curious onlookers. With support from Ms. Rashid, in a span of a few months, they had reframed teaching and learning for their classes. They created a team approach to instruction and were allowed to combine two classes. Although they often disagreed about how to proceed, they never once criticized each other personally. The principal always kept them focused on the ultimate goal: building and sustaining a community in which learning was valued above all else.

Pulling It Together in the Classroom

The sixth-grade class in "Issues and Perspectives" is taught by a team of four teachers, one each from language arts, social studies, fine arts, and career development. The students have been examining the topic "Messages Images Tell" and have just completed an assignment of "Personal Images of the United States," in which they created visual representations of their perceptions of the country. Their products are now on display around the room, and an exploration of them is about to begin. The range, variety, and richness of the images are breathtaking: a 24" x 36" photograph of a biracial, multiethnic student in class, with the caption, "I am what America is and has the potential to be"; a drawing of a multigenerational Native American family bowed down from carrying a model of the United States on their backs; a drawing of many different people, all wearing various sets of numbers; a poster of eight naked babies from different ethnic groups; a collage showing teeming buildings of steel that seem to grow out of garbage dumps. Yet another picture shows individuals in silhouette looking at a map of the United States from the four cardinal directions—there is nothing on the inside of the map but big question marks. And there are many other images as well.

The classroom is alive with energy, excitement, anticipation, and free-flowing conversation. The students can hardly wait for the structured dialogue to begin. The teacher appeals to them to wait until he dispenses with some administrative tasks. Once these are completed, he announces, "Let us begin. . . ." This invitation is met with a barrage of thoughts, opinions, feelings, interpretations, comparisons, speculations, and throughout it all, pride, critique, discovery, insight, and celebration of accomplishment.

In the midst of these exuberant exchanges, Ms. Rashid, Dr. Carroll, two school board members, and a few Fieldston teachers enter the room. With an air of expectation, they listen to the level of conversation and take in the display of images. The teaching team member who had the primary responsibility for facilitating the class dialogue on the images sits and listens to the students present their projects. He smiles rather coyly, with pleasure and pride about what is happening. . . .

One Year Later . . .

Fieldston Middle School is well on its way to forging a learning community that values curriculum experimentation and instructional innovation. In a very short time, with administrative support and modeling at the district and building levels, Fieldston teachers realize first-hand that a community of learning is comprised of members who can

- share ideas and learn from one another;
- support one another through more collaborative practices in meetings and inside classrooms (e.g., peer coaching, mentoring, and other processes that promote sustained growth);

- accept divergent points of view, agree to "disagree" with one another in nonjudgmental ways, and come to consensus whenever possible; and
- enter into dialogue with one another, using reflective practice to examine issues that matter most to the school.

Reflective Questions

1. Have you experienced a situation in any way similar to the one in the case? Describe or explain.

2. How does this case study represent the main ideas presented in this book?

3. Can you identify the strategies discussed in this book that were applied in the case? Explain.

4. What other strategies might have been employed?

5. What challenges in the case presented the most difficulty for you personally?

6. What steps will likely be taken to expand the curriculum renewal process at Fieldston?

7. What might other schools in the district learn from the Fieldston model?

8. If you became principal of a school that had no idea about establishing a learning community, what first steps would you take?

9. What challenges would you anticipate, similar to or different from the ones in the case?

10. Describe specific strategies for each of the following stages:
    a. Initiating a learning community
    b. Supporting a learning community
    c. Sustaining a learning community
    d. Assessing a learning community

11. What resources (personnel or otherwise) would you need to accomplish each stage above?

12. What more do you need to know to get started establishing or sustaining a learning community?

Conclusion

From our experience, many schools are far from being optimal learning communities. Sometimes individuals are not committed to the concept out of ignorance or simply lack the insight and visionary leadership to make it a reality. Other challenges arise out of economic, social, organizational, or political factors that serve as an impenetrable and proverbial "monolithic steel monster" to preclude the establishment of a learning community. We believe that initiating, supporting, and sustaining learning communities are moral imperatives for educational leaders. We believe in the enormous personal and spiritual power of the individual to overcome the obstacles that thwart efforts to achieve high achievement for all children. We encourage readers to apply the techniques in this book to make learning communities a reality. Although the case presented in this chapter discussed some challenges to building learning communities, for the most part, it described a success story. More often than not, leaders make mistakes. The key to success, though, as trite as it may sound, is to persevere. Making mistakes and even the occasional failure lead the way to success. Every successful leader has erred along the way. Those who surrender to mishaps or outright failure never realize the golden opportunities they missed. Maintain and trust your perspective and belief system. Success doesn't occur overnight. As Dr. Carroll might suggest: Stay the course.

Resource

The Problematic Student

Step 1: Identify a Problematic Student

Think of a student who is problematic to you, that is, one whose current behavior presents a gap with some image of how you would like this person to behave in the role of student. Before doing any observation—and don't cheat on this—write down a description of the problematic behavior as you perceive it. Also indicate how you would like the student to be.

Step 2: Observe

Observe carefully the student's actual behavior in as many settings for as much time as you can arrange. Aside from the classroom, good places to observe include the playground and the lunchroom. Extracurricular activities offer another opportunity to observe behavior. For classroom observations, you may gather information about the student in your own class, but it is better to observe in classroom settings that differ from your own, in method or subject area. Record as accurately as you are able the actual behaviors you observe. These should be as close to facts as you can get. Facts are those descriptions that a group of reasonable and carefully observant individuals could agree on.

Step 3: Analyze

Describe the learning that you came to about the student, yourself, and your mental models. Look for discrepancy between what you knew about the student and what you saw. Wrestle with what this tells you about yourself, especially your mental models. (If you want to be really reflective, go back to your platform statement and take a look at what you intend to do.) Indicate any other learning you came to in the process of moving toward enhanced personal leadership and ability to model new ways of thinking and doing that lead toward improving education for kids.

References

Arbuckle, M. A., & Murray, L. B. (1989). *Building systems for professional growth: An action guide.* Andover, MA: Regional Laboratory for Educational Improvement of the Northeast and Islands.

Baum, W. M. (1994). *Understanding behaviorism: Science, behavior, and culture.* New York: HarperCollins.

Beebe, S. A., & Masterson, J. T. (2000). *Communicating in small groups* (6th ed.). New York: Longman.

Bennis, W. (1989). *On becoming a leader.* Reading, MA: Addison-Wesley.

Bolman, L. G., & Deal, T. E. (2002). *Reframing the path to school leadership: A guide for teachers and principals.* Thousand Oaks, CA: Corwin.

Bolton, R. (1979). *People skills.* New York: Simon & Schuster.

Bridges, E. (1992). *Problem-based learning for administrators.* Eugene, OR: ERIC Clearinghouse on Educational Management, University of Oregon.

Brown, J. S., & Duguid, P. (2000). *The social life of information.* Cambridge, MA: Harvard Business School Press.

Bryson, B. (2003). *A short history of nearly everything.* New York: Broadway.

Buckingham, M., & Clifton, D. O. (2001). *Now, discover your strengths.* New York: Free Press.

Cushman, K. (1996). Looking collaboratively at student work: An essential toolkit. *Horace, 13*(2), 7. Coalition of Essential Schools. Providence, RI: Brown University.

Daresh, J. C. (1996, April). *Lessons for educational leadership from career preparation in law, medicine, and training for the priesthood.* Paper presented at the Annual Meeting of the American Educational Research Association, New York.

Dewey, J. (1938). *Experience and education.* New York: Macmillan.

Doyle, M., & Straus, D. (1982). *How to make meetings work.* New York: Jove Books.

Drucker, P. F. (1999). *Management challenges for the 21st century.* New York: Harper Business.

Dunn, D. (1995). *Exploring social relationships.* Englewood Cliffs, NJ: Prentice Hall.

Elliott, D., & McKenney, M. (1998). Four inclusion models that work. *Teaching Exceptional Children, 30*(4), 54–58.

Elmore, R. (2003). The problem of stakes in performance-based accountability systems. In S. Fuhrman & R. Elmore (Eds.), *Redesigning accountability systems.* New York: Teachers College Press.

Evans, R. (2004). *Family matters: How schools can cope with the crisis of child-rearing.* San Francisco: Jossey-Bass.

Fosnot, C. (1989). *Enquiring teachers, enquiring learners: A constructivist approach to teaching.* New York: Teachers College Press.

Fosnot, C. T. (1993). *In search of understanding the case for constructivist classrooms.* Alexandria, VA: Association for Supervision and Curriculum Development.

Fullan, M. (1997). *What's worth fighting for in the principalship.* New York: Teachers College Press.

Fullan, M. (1999). *Change forces: The sequel.* Philadelphia: Falmer Press.

Fullan, M. (Ed.). (2000). *The Jossey-Bass reader on educational leadership.* San Francisco: Jossey-Bass.

Fullan, M. (2003). *Change forces with a vengeance.* London: RoutledgeFalmer.

Gardner, H. (1995). *Leading minds: An anatomy of leadership.* New York: Basic Books.

Gladwell, M. (2000). *The tipping point.* Boston: Little, Brown.

Glanz, J. (2002). *Finding your leadership style: A guide for educators.* Alexandria, VA: Association for Supervision and Curriculum Development.

Glasser, W. (1999). *Choice theory: A new psychology of personal freedom.* New York: Perennial Current.

Goodlad, J. I., & McMannon, T. J. (Eds.). (1997). *The public purpose of education and schooling.* San Francisco: Jossey-Bass.

Green, R. L. (2005). *Practicing the art of leadership: A problem-based approach to implementing the ISLLC standards* (2nd ed.). Columbus, OH: Pearson Merrill Prentice Hall.

Grossman, P., Wineburg, S., & Woolworth, S. (2001). Toward a theory of teacher community. *Teachers College Record, 103,* 942–1012.

Hansen, J. H., & Lifton, E. (1999). *Leadership for continuous school improvement.* Swampscott, MA: Watersun.

Hargreaves, A., & Fullan, M. (1998). *What's worth fighting for out there?* New York: Teachers College Press.

Harris, S. (2004). *The end of faith: Religion, terror, and the future of reason.* New York: Norton.

Herszenhorn, D. M. (2004, April 7). Studies in Chicago fault policy of holding back third graders. *New York Times,* p. B1.

Herszenhorn, D. M., & Gootman, E. (2004, April 19). City tests loom and third graders feel the heat. *New York Times,* pp. B1, B2.

Himley, M. (with Carfini, P. F.). (2000). *From another angle: Children's strengths and school standards.* New York: Teachers College Press.

Howard, J. (1987). *The Efficacy Institute, Inc.* Lexington, MA: Author.

Hurston, Z. N. (1996). *Complete stories.* New York: HarperCollins.

Johnston, C. A. (1996). *Unlocking the will to learn.* Thousand Oaks, CA: Corwin.

Johnston, C. A. (1998). *Let me learn.* Thousand Oaks, CA: Corwin.

Johnston, C. A. (2004a). *Learning to use my potential.* Paper presented at the Pioneer Leadership Academy, University of Houston, TX, June 16–20.

Johnston, C. A. (2004b). *When you are ready to begin to make a difference.* Annual ASAH Conference, State of New Jersey, Atlantic City, November 12.

Johnston, C. A. (2005). *Power by design.* Paper presented at the EU-Sponsored Meeting of the Grundtvig Partnership, Westminster University, London, January 9–11.

Johnston, C. A., & Dainton, G. (1997). *The learning combination inventory.* Pittsgrove, NJ: Let Me Learn, Inc.

Kochhar, C. A., West, L. L., & Taymans, J. M. (2000). *Successful inclusion: Practical strategies for a shared responsibility.* Upper Saddle River, NJ: Merrill.

Korzybski, A. (1995). *Science and sanity* (5th ed.). Lakeville, CT: International Non-Aristotelian Library. (Original work published 1933)

Lambert, L., Walker, D., Zimmerman, D. P., Cooper, J. E., Lambert, M. D., Gardner, M. E., & Szabo, M. (2003). *The constructivist leader* (2nd ed.). New York: Teachers College Press.

Maxcy, S. J. (2002). *Ethical school leadership.* Lanham, MD: Scarecrow.

McDonald, J. P., Mohr, N., Dichter, A., & McDonald, E. C. (2003). *The power of protocols.* New York: Teachers College Press.

McLeskey, J., & Waldron, N. (2001). *Inclusive schools in action: Making differences ordinary.* Alexandria, VA: Association for Supervision and Curriculum Development.

Meyers, I. B., & McCaulley, M. H. (1985). *Manual: A guide to the development and use of the Myers-Briggs Type Indicator.* Palo Alto, CA: Consulting Psychologists Press.

Morse, T. E. (2002). Designing appropriate curriculum for special education students in urban schools. *Education and Urban Schools, 35,* 4–17.

Moxley, R. S. (2000). *Leadership and spirit: Breathing new vitality and quality into individuals and organizations.* San Francisco: Jossey-Bass.

Nadelstern, E., Price, J. R., & Listhaus, A. (2000). Student empowerment through the professional development of teachers. In J. Glanz & L. S. Behar-Horenstein (Eds.), *Paradigm debates in curriculum and supervision: Modern and postmodern perspectives* (pp. 265–275). Westport, CT: Bergin & Garvey.

Neusner, J. (2003). *World religions in America: An introduction.* Westminster, UK: John Knox Press.

Null, G. (1996). *Who are you, really? Understanding your life's quality.* New York: Carroll & Graf.

Osterman, K. E., & Kottkamp, R. B. (1993). *Reflective practice for educators: Improving schooling through professional development.* Thousand Oaks, CA: Corwin.

Osterman, K. E., & Kottkamp, R. B. (2004). *Reflective practice for educators: Professional development to improve student learning* (2nd ed.). Thousand Oaks, CA: Corwin.

Patterson, J. L. (1993). *Leadership for tomorrow's schools.* Alexandria, VA: Association for Supervision and Curriculum Development.

Philip, H. (1936). *An experimental study of the frustration of will-acts and conation.* Cambridge, UK: Cambridge University Press.

Piaget, J., & Inhelder, B. (1971). *The psychology of the child.* New York: Basic Books.

Quick, P. M., & Normore, A. H. (2004). Moral leadership for the 21st century. *The Educational Forum, 68,* 336–347.

Roberts, S., & Pruitt, E. (2003). *Schools as professional learning communities.* Thousand Oaks, CA: Corwin.

Schon, D. A. (1983). *The reflective practitioner: How professionals think in action.* New York: Basic Books.

Schon, D. A. (1984). Leadership as reflection-in-action. In T. J. Sergiovanni & J. E. Corbally (Eds.), *Leadership and organizational culture: New perspectives on administrative theory and practice* (pp. 36–63). Urbana: University of Illinois Press.

Schon, D. A. (1987). *Educating the reflective practitioner: Toward a new design for thinking and learning in the professional.* San Francisco: Jossey-Bass.

Schussler, D. L. (2003). Schools as learning communities: Unpacking the concept. *Journal of School Leadership, 13,* 498–528.

Seligman, M. (1998). *Learned optimism.* New York: Free Press.

Senge, P. M. (1990). *The fifth discipline: The art and practice of the learning organization.* New York: Doubleday.

Senge, P. M., Cambron-McCabe, N., Lucas, T., Smith, B., Dutton, J., & Kleiner, A. (2000). *Schools that learn: The fifth discipline fieldbook for educators, parents, and everyone who cares about education.* New York: Doubleday-Currency.

Senge, P., Kleiner, A., Roberts, C., Ross, R. B., & Smith, B. (1994). *A fifth discipline fieldbook for educators, parents, and everyone who cares about education.* New York: Doubleday.

Sergiovanni, T. J. (1992). *Moral leadership: Getting to the heart of school improvement.* San Francisco: Jossey-Bass.

Sergiovanni, T J. (1994a). *Building community in schools: Leadership for the schoolhouse.* San Francisco: Jossey-Bass.

Sergiovanni, T. J. (1994b). Organizations or communities? Changing the metaphor changes the theory. *Educational Administration Quarterly, 30,* 214–226.

Sergiovanni, T. J. (1996). *Leadership for the schoolhouse: How is it different? Why is it important?* San Francisco: Jossey-Bass.

Sergiovanni, T. J. (2000). *The lifeworld of leadership: Creating culture, community, and personal meaning in our schools.* San Francisco: Jossey-Bass.

Serpell, R. (1993). Interface between sociocultural and psychological aspects of cognition. In E. Forman, N. Minick, & C. A. Stone (Eds.), *Contexts for learning: Sociocultural dynamics in children's development* (pp. 357–368). New York: Oxford University Press.

Skinner, B. F. (1976). *Walden two.* Englewood Cliffs, NJ: Prentice Hall.

Sowell, T. (1996). *Migration and culture.* New York: Basic Books.

Sowell, T. (2002). *A conflicting vision: Ideological origins of political struggles.* New York: Basic Books.

Sowell, T. (2003). *Basic economics.* New York: Basic Books.

Stacey, R. (2001). *Complex responsive processes in organizations.* London: Routledge.

Starratt, R. J. (2003). A perspective on ethical educational leadership: An ethics of presence. In F. C. Lunenburg & C. S. Carr (Eds.), *Shaping the future: Policy, partnerships, and emerging perspectives.* Lanham, MD: Scarecrow Education.

Steinhauer, J. (2004, April 8). Mayor says prevention is key in plan to hold back students. *New York Times*, p. B3.

Sullivan, S., & Glanz, J. (2005). *Supervision that improves teaching: Strategies and techniques* (2nd ed.). Thousand Oaks, CA: Corwin.

Von Glasersfeld, E. (1997). Amplification of a constructivist perspective. *Issues in Education, 3,* 203–210.

Vygotsky, L. S. (1978). *Mind in society: The development of higher mental process.* Boston, MA: Harvard University Press.

Vygotsky, L. S. (1986). *Thought and language.* (Ed. and Trans., Alex Kozulin). Cambridge: MIT Press. (Original work published 1934)

Weiss, J. (1997). *Ideology of death: Why the holocaust happened in Germany.* New York: Ivan R. Dee.

Wenger, E., McDermott, R., & Snyder, W. (2002). *Cultivating communities of practice.* Boston: Harvard Business School Press.

Westheimer, J. (1999). Communities and consequences: An inquiry into ideology and practice in teachers' professional work. *Educational Administration Quarterly, 35,* 71–105.

Winerip, M. (2004a, April 28). Making leaps but still labeled as failing. *New York Times*, p. B9.

Winerip, M. (2004b, April 4). Principal sees mistake in plan to hold back third graders. *New York Times*, p. B9.

Wolfendale, S. (2000). *Special needs in the early years: Snapshots of practice.* London: Routledge.

Woolfolk, A., & Hoy, W. K. (2003). *Instructional leadership: A learning-centered guide.* Boston: Allyn & Bacon.

Zepeda, S. (2000). *Instructional supervision: Applying tools and concepts.* Larchmont, NY: Eye on Education.

Index